Sex Talk: Discussions with Prostitutes, Porn Stars, Producers, Photographers and Penmen

Rockit Reports

Contents

Introduction

I go by the name of Rockit. I'm called that because I like to blast off. You may know me from my previous books. You may know me from my website. Or you may not know me at all.

For those who fall into the latter category, allow me to make a bit of an introduction. Over the last few decades I have made my way around the world and back, several times over. Along the way I have come into close contact with the commercial sex industry. This led to as much education as enjoyment.

Several years ago, I started a website to share some of the knowledge I gained in the hopes that it would entertain whoever came across it. I had no idea how popular the website would become. With a healthy readership I decided to publish my first book just over a year after starting the website. That was followed by the original version of the book that you now hold in your hands.

Today my website is viewed by millions annually. Through everything that's gone on, and with the help of continued travel and today's ever present social media, I have come in contact with a variety of people who work in or around the commercial sex industry.

This book contains a collection of interviews with some of those people, who range from professional porn stars and paid penis polishers to producers and erotica authors.

These interviews are presented as they were done, with only some light editing for clarity. I truly hope you will enjoy.

Porn Star Tia Ling

Tia Ling is a pretty well-known Asian-American porn star. Besides being very hot, her story is interesting since she started as a swinger and got into porn with her husband's support.

How old are you and how and when did you get into porn?

I'm 36 now. I started when I was 28

When did you watch your first porn? Do you remember it?

Honestly I have no idea, haha. It was probably with my current husband then boyfriend.

You have said before that you were into swinging before you got into porn. How did that start? Does your husband bang other girls when you're not around, or is it only when you are together?

We only did things together, but yeah it all started with him. Mostly my fantasy of having a multiple guy scenario.

If you could start over again would you still have gotten into porn?

Yes and no …. I've enjoyed my experiences but there's definitely some drawbacks to being in adult.

Do you think sex addiction is real?

No not really …. I mean you can love sex, but I'm not really sure how you could be addicted to it. Everyone just has different sex drives I think.

If you had all the money you could ever want or need, would you have done porn?

Yes I would have just for certain sexual fantasy experiences, but I probably wouldn't have done as long as I have.

Have you had any issues with family or friends finding out about your adult work? Has it caused any problems in your personal life?

I've been pretty lucky that none of my family has found out and I really don't keep in touch with most of my high school friends. Many people at the college I recently graduated from found out, but luckily it hasn't really caused any problems.

What would your advice be to a person wanting to follow in your footsteps? How about if it was a sister of yours? Would that change things?

Things are a lot different now in porn than when I first stated. At this point you really can't think of porn as a possible full time career. More of a side career or second job, unless you happen to be one of the very few that takes off like Asa [Akira]. But most girls coming in these days don't get the volume of work we used to get when I first started. Not as much work, twice as many girls, fewer companies and too much free porn.

Do you watch porn now that you make it? Who is your favorite porn star of all time? Favorite source of porn?

Yes I do. We watch a lot of my scenes together, haha, but my favorite other than myself to watch would probably be Asa,

India Summer.

What do you think of prostitution? What about porn stars who escort?

I don't have a problem with girls who do, but it's not something that's for me.

Have you ever stripped or done adult webcamming? What do you think of them?

I started as a dancer before porn so yes. I've done some camming for my website and/or private shows. Both can be fun.

What was the worst shoot you've done? How was it shooting with Kink? Facial Abuse?

Either facial abuse or this live shoot I did for a fetish company in NY … same guys that do hardtied.com. It was just way over the top, as was FA. Kink is actually a lot of fun the way they shoot. It just looks a lot worse than it really is, haha.

Is it true that most porn stars make more from side work like feature dancing and appearances than actual scenes?

They can yes, especially these days. Feature dancing can be very good.

What was your earliest sexual experience with a woman?

Not until porn actually. I couldn't even tell you who my first girl was with at this point, haha.

What's the craziest sexual thing you've done?

Hard to say at this point, but probably a 10 guy gang bang I did in my personal life.

Ever walk in on your parents having sex?

Haha … no thank god.

Spit or swallow?

Swallow, but I'll spit / drool if the guy likes to see it coming from my mouth!

Worst job you've ever had?

Dancing before porn. I really hated it.

I remember seeing some awesome videos of you lactating. Did you do any shoots while pregnant? Did your implants interfere with your pregnancy at all?

The implants actually didn't interfere at all. I didn't do any preggo shoots.

Rather take a cock down your throat or up your ass?

Actually both at the same time, haha.

Are you often recognized on the street? How is that?

Yes I have been. It's kind of awkward for me really, I don't like that kind of attention.

How is it meeting fans who have jacked off over you countless times? Ever have any problems with creepy fans?

Most fans are very sweet and nice …. but of course you meet some creepy ones too. Can't say I've really ever had any serious problems though.

If you're out on your own for the day with no plan of having sex or being seen unclothed what kind of panties do you wear?

I wear thongs most of the time.

How long will you continue in the adult industry? What other plans do you have for the future?

Well, I'm actually retired for the most part at this point. I've started a full time job as an interior designer, just finished school last December. But I'm still continuing with my site for the moment, just not shooting in LA anymore.

Any last words?

It's been a great ride (no pun intended, haha).

Cam Model Bella French

Bella French is a big breasted blond webcam model that I first encountered online. It didn't take long to find out that she used to work as a dancer and an escort in Canada and had lived a pretty interesting life. I contacted her for an interview.

How and when did you get into webcamming, stripping and making sex videos? Which was first?

I started as a stripper for a very short period of time. I did not like the fact that I had to work at night, and being surrounded by alcohol and drugs. I wanted to do something else and that is how I discovered webcamming. I started webcamming in November 2011 on MyFreeCams. I had no experience at all and completely fell in love with it. In July 2012, I filmed my first solo masturbation video and until today I love being in front of the cam.

What's your best sexual memory? What's your worst?

My best sexual memory is the first time I had an orgasm with my first boyfriend. I was 15. I did not understand what was going on, but while it was happening the feeling was amazing. Since that moment I have been wanting it every day.

My worst sexual experience was when I got raped. That is how I lost my virginity. It was a bad experience, but I have grown from it, and it made me a stronger person.

If you could start over again would you still have gotten into the adult industry? If you were born with all the money you

ever needed would you have done it?

I would definitely do it again. Since I was very young I have always felt that the porn stars were the coolest and hottest girls out there. What I like about webcamming is that I can make my own schedule, and I'm 100 percent independent financially. What brought me to this industry was the fact that I needed financial help to avoid bankruptcy from a previous business. Of course, if money was not an issue I would not have done it.

How many men have you fucked in your life?

Honestly not that many. I have mostly been in relationships, and I never cheated on my boyfriends. Because of rough times, I became an escort and that boosted my number.

Your tits and very large and very amazing. When did you get them done? How was it?

Thank you so much! I had three breast enlargement surgeries. Before getting implants, I had a small C cup and I upgraded that to 450cc implants. Six months later, I wanted to go bigger so I decided to go up to 800cc. One year after that, I noticed that one of my implants was lower, therefore I decided to have a third surgery going up to 1200cc. It's a painful operation, but the pain disappears as soon as you look at yourself in the mirror.

What are the best and worst things that have come out of your adult industry experiences? Has anything ever made you want to quit?

I would have to say that the best thing is the fans. They are always so nice and amazing. They make this whole webcam experience positive and make me want to give more.

Of course there are the haters, and when you're tired or having a bad day, it's really hard to get insulted over and over again. Sometimes some guys don't realize that cam girls and porn stars are humans and not only sex machines.

Do you prefer dancing on stage, performing on webcam or making videos? Which one earns the most money?

I love them all the same. If I had an offer to dance in one of Montreal's strip clubs once a week I would do it. I'm an exhibitionist and I love to get naked and perform. I believe that if you're an amazing stripper you make more money than an average webcam girl and vice versa.

How long do you plan on gracing the world with your awesome cam shows, videos and pictures? What are your plans for the future?

I love what I do, and have no intentions of leaving this industry as long as the fans will come in my room and see me perform. For the future, I'm hoping to do more modeling for magazines and keep adding content to my website.

Have you had any issues with family or friends finding out about your adult work? Has it caused any problems in your personal life?

I have not been in contact with my family for years, and that was way before I started webcamming. They were against my decision of getting bigger boobs. As for my friends, only two of them know what I do. If it stays this way it's all good. Let's see for the future.

What would your advice be to a person wanting to follow in your footsteps? How about if it was a sister of yours? What that change things?

The first thing to keep in mind is to always have fun. Never do what you're not comfortable doing. Be surrounded with people that are positive. If I had a sister and if that's what she wanted to do, I would want her to do better than me. I would promote her all the time.

Would you say the average cam girl makes more or less money over their career than they would have if they done a "vanilla" job (notice I said average and not a standout girl like you)?

I think it would be about the same, but if your comfortable doing webcamming there are so many more advantages (you make your own schedule, you work from home, you're your own boss, etc.).

Do you watch porn? Who is your favorite porn star of all time?

Yes, I love watching porn when I see that the girl is enjoying herself. It gets me excited when I watch Jenna Jameson, she is my ultimate fantasy.

What do you think of prostitution? Would you ever do it?

I have done it in the past, but it was elite escorting. I think it is very dangerous, and the key is to be surrounded with a professional agency.

Cock or pussy?

I'm all about cock, but having a pussy once in a while always makes me happy.

Spit or swallow?

I like a clean job so I'll go with swallow.

What do you think of cum shots on the face?

Yes please! Love it!

Have you ever met one of your cam fans? If so, how was it?

Yes I have met the winner of my date raffle, and we had an amazing time here in Montreal. I about to meet the winner of my second date raffle.

What is your favorite book? Favorite movie? Favorite city?

"The End of Over Eating," *The Dark Knight*, Montreal.

When your home alone, what do you wear?

Nothing… Sweat pants and hoodies.

Any final words for my readers?

Thank you for taking the time to read this. I hope you enjoyed reading this as much as I enjoyed this interview. Big kisses from your naughty Montreal cam girl.

Erotica Author Jay Walken

Jay Walken has written a number of erotica titles that are set in around the sex scene in Southeast Asia. It should be obvious why I had an interest in this author and his works.

Where are you from?

The United States. New York.

When did you first come to Southeast Asia?

When I was 35.

When did you first procure the services of a prostitute?

I don't use the word "prostitution" to describe every exchange of sex in return for money or some other form of reward, including a hoped for promotion. In every sex act, there is something that one partner expects from the other–whether pleasure, or a promise or hope of love, or financial security, or a long term commitment. There are women who think like prostitutes, for whom the act is nothing but an exchange of pussy for money; I never repeat a sexual act with such a woman. But to answer your question, in my early twenties, when I was in a strange foreign city.

How has Southeast Asia changed since your first visit? How have you changed?

It has lost some of its innocence and openness, I think. I accept it for what it is: I am not as surprised as I was at first by what I found there.

What do you think about prostitution?

As I answered in the earlier question, I also think of politicians who sell their integrity for money as prostitutes, as more egregious prostitutes than those who give some happiness to lonely men.

Do you have any interest in Western women today?

Sure I do. But only a certain type.

When did you start writing, and why?

In my teens. It just came naturally to me.

What advice to you have for someone making their first trip to Southeast Asia in search of sexual services?

Turn around, unless you respect women, and can treat them as human beings, regard each person as unique.

In your opinion, what is the best book you've written?

"Erotic Adventure in Thailand," and "Milk and Pussy in Indonesia"–they both have the kind of humor and occasionally inspired writing that I cherish in other writers.

What is the best book ever written about Southeast Asia and/or sex?

I can't answer this, but "Tropic of Cancer" is a beauty.

What advice to you have to aspiring writers?

Read the kind of writers you would like to become; and also read others, be open-minded and omnivorous. Because, once you actually begin to write, you may not find much time to read other writers, or wish to lose your originality by unconsciously imitating the writers you have just read.

Porn Producer Morshe

There is more pornography out there today than any one person could ever watch. Only some of it stands out from the pack. Morshe produces high quality porn with beautiful women in Thailand that is then sold on the internet.

How and when did you get into porn? Is the kind of Thai content you do now what you started out with?

It was suggested that I do it some 12 years ago by a friend. He wanted to make money with the business. I kept it in mind and bought a camera that was meant for shoots. I did amateur stuff in my room just as a hobby. The guy who suggested doing porn left Thailand in 2003 and never returned so I put the business on the back burner. Later on I ended up working with some guys doing porn here in Thailand introduced by a girl I had known who called me up out of the blue back in 2004. She asked if I was interested in doing some performer work on shoots. So I eventually got into the director role and that's what I do now. The content I do now is very similar to what I started out with.

Do you shoot in Thailand because it's cheaper, more fun or for some other reason?

I've been here for so long whore mongering that I decided to make a business out of it. That's the reason and not the cheaper or more fun reasons.

When did you first travel to Thailand? How did you find about the commercial sex scene there? How has the country

changed since your first visit?

I first came to Thailand in the mid to late 90's, the commercial sex scene was alive and kicking then as it is now. The country has become much more expensive over the years. The girls are less likely to go long time and the prices have gone up for girls especially in the last 3-5 years.

Have you been to any other countries known for their sex industry like say the Philippines? How did you like them? How do you think they compare to the Thailand?

I have been to the Philippines for whore mongering. I like the girls attitudes a bit better in the Philippines as well as the girls in the scene tend to be a few years younger on average. The girls tend to be slightly less attractive, but that's probably because they get fat a bit quicker then the Thai's do. That place has gotten more expensive as well and at this point it's no longer cheaper to choose Angeles over Pattaya. So I probably won't be back there but once every other year.

What is your first sexual memory? What is your best?

Not sure about this one. Nothing interesting comes to mind.

What was the first porn you saw?

I think it was *Loose Ends* part 2 with Erica Boyer who I thought was very hot at the time. Probably 1986-7.

What is the biggest inconvenience of making your porn flicks?

Looking for girls, a "coalition of the willing" if you will. I was just looking for girls last night and no takers. If you lower your standards you'll find girls all the time.

If you could start over again would you still have done porn? Do the benefits outweigh the costs?

I'm not sure I would do porn again, it's been very hard work and has yet to really pay off. There are things I really like about it, like shagging the girls when I get the chance but that's usually off scene. I think this question is still in flux and still yet to be determined.

Have you had any issues with family or friends finding out about your adult work? Has it caused any problems in your personal life?

Oh yeah. Family disapproves. Most don't seem to care but some vocal members are quite irate. Not a huge personal problem as I'm out of sight out of mind for the most part.

How difficult is it to find models? Is it more difficult now than it used to be? Some producers say the prices women want to model are rising and the amount they can actually make from the shoots are falling to the point where it almost doesn't make sense to even make porn anymore. What do you say about that?

This kind of touches on things I've mentioned above. It's quite difficult to find models unless you lower your standards. It's always been quite difficult to find models for as long as I've been working, since 2006 at least, now as difficult as then but I wouldn't say more. I heard that it was quite easy before 2004. I don't think the prices for models are rising. As for the not making enough money to produce porn, it does seem that way. It really has been a struggle.

How do you deal with things like the increase of prices for sex services in Thailand, the conservatism of many Thai women when it comes to things like doing anal or even blow

jobs, and the increase in internet awareness that has many Thai sex workers refusing to take any kind of sexual pictures or video?

The increase of price of sexual services, I suspect, that the girls are going with less customers but at a higher price. This is more a personal problem then it is with the porn business. The blow job problem hasn't come up too many times so it's rare we get a girl that won't do a BJ. Anal is always difficult to get. On the problems with girls worried about being on the internet, you just have to ask so many more until you get a taker.

Are most of the girls you shoot with pro prostitutes, semi-pros or total amateurs? Have any run into problems after being in your movies?

It's a mix of the 3. As for them running into problems, quite a few have had problems being seen on the internet but that's usually because somebody showed them their picture rather then themselves or a family member having stumbled upon it.

Sometimes a guy will take a girl back to his room only to find out that things are a little fishy downstairs. Do you ever get a model who smells so bad that you've canceled a shoot?

No, never so bad that we had to cancel. The reason's you would have to have to cancel on similar reasons would be if the girl had some weird growths or scars that were unable to be hidden. Most girls know the score better and won't attempt the scene with out having some faith in their body's appearance.

I've read that some guys who shot in Thailand but didn't hide their identities have actually been banned from reentering the country. What about that?

Never heard of that. It might be the case but I can't confirm that.

What do you think about prostitution and pornography in general?

Prostitution is perfectly fine in my book. This wasn't always the case but as I got out of my teen years I realized how similar prostitution is to any relationship. The woman expects a provider and that's what she gets. Prostitution gives her a moment's provider but with less emotional baggage for both parties. The man receives sexual services at the least and sometimes a very girl friend like experience. Pornography seems fine, it is very powerful imagery that incites the senses.

How do you think porn can continue to be profitable with all of the free content now available online? Has the advent of file sharing, tube sites and the like put a big dent in your earnings?

I think advertisers are going to have to take on the costs of producing porn. That or Kickstarter campaigns where the people who are fans of your work will pitch in donations for scenes. So the scenes will be paid for before the shoot. Free has hurt the industry and the business model will have to change going forward.

What is the last book you read? What is your favorite book?

Stephen King's "Wind Through The Keyhole." I don't know if it's my favorite but very apropos of the times we live in is "1984."

To wrap up, thanks a lot for taking the time to answer these questions. Is there anything you'd like to say to readers.

We've worked really hard on AsianCandyPop and I hope you guys appreciate it. Even if you can't put any money to the cause, we just want to make Asian porn better. It really is a labor of love.

Cam Model Mila Milan

Mila Milan is another webcam model I discovered online. Her story is particularly interesting. She is European but is based in Southeast Asia. She is also involved in a number of things outside of webcamming, from furniture to design to investment.

How old are you?

25.

When did you have sex the first time? When did you see your first porn?

At 16, on a school trip in Austria. It was very 'hairy.'

When was your first sexual experience with a woman?

16.

How did you get into the adult industry? What was your first adult job?

I made some German spoken Porn at a very young age, haha, but really started professionally at 21.

Which adult job do you like most: webcam, making movies, or something else?

I like to cam. It is much more difficult than shooting movies. In movies you get directions: do this, do that. On cam you really

27

have to be an entertainer and keep the room busy.

Very few porn stars are good cam girls and few cam girls do porn.

Do you prefer women or men?

Really depends on the person, but I've only had males as a serious partner in life

What do you think about prostitution?

I have a lot of respect for the girls and women working in prostitution. Living part of my yearly life in Asia I see from close how hard that kind of work is. I have no negative view of the business but I just know that it is extremely hard work. Were I do have a problem with is underage prostitution and trafficking. Prostitution as your own choice fine, forced prostitution: castrate them ....

What is your favorite book? Favorite movie?

Ouch ...so many books: but .. "Die Verwandlung" (Metamorphosis) – Franz Kafka is amongst the contenders for #1. Movies: *9 1/2 Weeks* (love Mickey Rourke pre-op) and *Equilibrium* (Mr. Bale yum yum).

You have been to many countries. Which is the best in your opinion?

I was born in Austria, lived in 7 different countries, and been to dozens. I love the US for its wideness, people, opportunities and just the feel of it. But my heart I lost to Thailand.

I will always be an Austrian born with a Thai heart.

Where did you meet those sexy Thai girls you perform on cam with? Do you have play with them off cam?

Haha, they are friends and they do this also next to their regular jobs. I play with girls also privately, yes not only bi for my image.

You are very interesting because you have diversified yourself into a number of industries like design, clothing, real estate and more. Which is your favorite? Which is your most successful?

I've always done several things at the same time, and have been doing design and painting large abstract pieces for almost a decade. I love the adult work, but I also love my fashion line, the lingerie and my Photography and Tattoo business. I make by far the most money in my design businesses (furniture, industrial, interiors), but am best known because of the cam work.

What are your plans for the future?

I have many many plans. First of all I set up a new holding were all my companies are brought into. I have sold almost 90% of the shares available in that (representing 1/4 of the total holding) and keep the rest in my name.

This will be the core of my new ventures. I am back on cam actively after the birth of my twin girls early February, and I will film a lot in the US this year. Along with the launch of my minimalist fashion line, the lingerie line I have developed will also be launched and we have the existing design business activities … I also will start tattooing again in the second half of the year. So many exciting things coming.

If you were born with all the money you could ever need, do

you think you would have got into the adult industry?

Yes. I was doing quite well in my design work and just needed an extra outlet for my energy. Adult work is a fun thing I do, not a need. The money is nice, but is not the sole reason to do it.

Porn Star Lana Violet

Lana Violet is an Asian-American porn actress in the United States that I've had my eye on for some time. She reminds me of a girl that I once knew.

I know you've answered this before, but for the benefit of my readers who don't know: How old are you and how and when did you get into porn?

I'm 24 now. I started porn in when I was 19. I stumbled upon the sexyjobs website and was looking into becoming a stripper. The majority of my offers were for adult work, so I made my way to the valley, met my first agent and just went for it. At first, I was still looking to just dance, but she convinced me I could make more doing videos so I tried it, liked it, and never looked back.

While the looks of most people, porn stars included, tend to diminish over time, you seem to actually get more beautiful and alluring as time goes on. What's your secret?

That's very kind thank you. I put effort in taking care of myself, making healthy dietary choices and practicing moderation. I don't drink as heavily as I did when I was younger that's for sure, and I do a lot of yoga that helps me in all kinds of ways. I've recently been getting into MMA which is really fun and challenging.

When did you watch your first porn? Do you remember it?

My first porn I really sat down to watch was what my agent first showed me; it was a bg [boy/girl] of one of her girls and Jack Napier. I never really sat down and watched a whole scene before, only saw trailers or random bits at friends' houses or parties.

What's your best sexual memory? What's your worst?

I couldn't point out one singular best sexual experience. My best memories are those involving two or more people.

If you could start over again would you still have gotten into porn?

Yes, no regrets. Regret is a hopeless emotion.

Do you think sex addiction is real?

I think addiction to anything is real, whether it be sex, drugs, food, pain, etc..

What would your advice be to a person wanting to follow in your footsteps?

Do your research, ask questions, don't be afraid to say no to doing something you're not comfortable with.

Do you watch porn now that you make it? Who is your favorite porn star of all time? Favorite source of porn?

Yea I'll watch porn here and there, more than I did before I got started. Favorite porn stars are Belladonna and Katsuni; I can watch scene after scene with either of them in it. Source would be the DVD's I own or buy usually.

Have you ever stripped or done adult webcamming? What do you think of them?

Stripped yes, webcamming yes. Stripping is fun I love to tease and dance around naked. Webcamming has it's perks, you're as personal with fans as you can get.

Is it true that most porn stars make more from side work like feature dancing and appearances than actual scenes?

I think it all depends on every girl and every situation.

What was your earliest sexual experience with a woman?

It was me, my guy friend, and my incredibly super sweet Canadian friend, who apparently had a wild side. We were all making out and we were fingering and licking each other.

Spit or swallow?

SWALLOW!

Rather take a cock down your throat or up your ass?

At the same time.

Are you often recognized on the street? How is that?

Not often, but I have been at least twice when I was working other jobs.

How is it meeting fans who have jacked off over you countless times? Ever have any problems with creepy fans?

It doesn't really faze me. That's the point to me, entertaining.

It's part of the business I'm in. Nothing too bad with creeper fans fortunately.

What is your favorite book? Favorite movie?

"Paradise Lost" by John Milton and *Fight Club*.

If you're out on your own for the day with no plan of having sex or being seen unclothed what kind of panties do you wear?

Haha, good question. The cheeky kind, where your under-ass shows. Not quite booty shorts and not quite a thong.

How long will you continue in the adult industry? What other plans do you have for the future?

I plan to take advantage of every opportunity that is presented to me, make the most of what I can when I can in this industry. I plan to open up my own site and shoot exclusive scenes there, and get into feature dancing more.

Any last words?

Huge thanks to all my fans and their support! Request me at your local club!

Author P.C. Anders

P.C. Anders is another author I came across online. His works really stood out because they are based around the global erotic massage scene. That's not a very common topic.

Where are you from?

The United States.

When did you first visit a massage parlor?

I received a massage from a woman who visited me at my place, bringing along her massage table—that was in Long Island, New York. Possibly the first "massage parlor" I visited, run by a Korean woman, was a few years later. It was in New York City.

If and when did you first get a "happy ending"? How did it go?

I got it from one of my first "licensed" therapists. Without asking my permission, she just picked up my penis and started running her hands up and down on it. I was surprised and just watched her do what she wanted to do, and it didn't take long for me to ejaculate, as I had been erect for half the massage! I would say that I found half the massage to be erotic, so the happy ending was just the icing on the cake.

How has massage changed over the years? How have you changed since first getting a massage?

There are many more varieties, and it is widely available. I remember I had to search a city up and down just to find a massage therapist and get an appointment. Now, it's a big business, and it's more respectable, unless it's not.

What do you think about erotic massage — ethically, legally, etc.?

I stand completely and unhesitatingly for individual freedom: so long both the giver and the receiver are consenting adults, it is no one's business to tell them what they can and can do. But if someone claims to be giving a professional massage, they need to be trained and be up to national standards, and not simply have some certificate from some vague outfit.

What kind of women are you interested in?

All kinds, if they are interested in me. But not masculine women—if you know what I mean. I like my women to be tender, gentle, relaxed, and have a sense of humor.

What advice to you have for someone making their first trip to a massage parlor?

I give lots of detailed advice in my two big books. In addition to explaining what I came across in different countries, and the learning experiences I had, here is an entire chapter of advice. Fundamentally, you need to know something about what to expect, and make clear what you want and what you are getting. Or you might be unpleasantly surprised or disappointed.

What's the best country for massage in your opinion?

It depends on what you're willing to pay. If money is no object, I think London, New York, Singapore, Hong Kong—they are all good. But the best value for your money, by far: I would say—Thailand, Indonesia, the Philippines, Cambodia. In general, Southeast Asia is such great value because of its combination of easygoing tolerance, a cultural acceptance of massage, both regular and erotic, and an abundant pool of qualified labor at low prices.

How popular are your books?

I would say "The Uncensored Massage: Thailand, Indonesia, Vietnam and China," has so far done the best, but the other books also contain gems, in my opinion.

Do you personally prefer paper or ebooks?

It's 50-50. I love the feel of paper, I love the ability to make markings, and to take a book along with me to the beach. On the other hand, I also appreciate the advantages of just taking along a 10-ounce Kindle on a trip, and having a thousand books inside it.

What is the best book ever written about massage and/or sex?

Honestly, I have not read any book about massage that is remotely like mine. I still doubt there is anyone who has received as many massages as I have: around 4,000, I think. I would say that Henry Miller's Tropic of Cancer and Tropic of Capricorn books are among the best books I have read that combine sex with literary value, character, and observation.

What advice do you have for aspiring writers?

Follow your dream, and realize it is more important to have fun and enjoy what you do than to make money. In fact, be aware that there is no direct connection between literary quality and money.

Porn Producer Shimmy

I first became aware of Shimmy when a porn website he made based on Native women began to make some news. Later he emerged with a website based on parts of the Dominican Republic famous for prostitution.

When did you first visit the Dominican Republic?

A few years ago.

When did you watch your first porn?

Around age 13 in the VHS tape days. I think it was called "Hometown Honeys.'

How did you get into porn?

Most everyone gets into porn accidentally. I went to school to be a programmer and as a side hustle I developed websites for local businesses back in the 90's to pay the bills. I did a few blog-style websites for fun and put up some porn banner ads and started slowly making a little money, which grew. Eventually I started my own adult sites purchasing and leasing content from other studios at the time, and in more recent years I got in front of the camera for a few studios as paid talent to fuck chicks and realized I had all the skills needed to be a one man show, from initial idea to filming to running the back end of the website, promoting it, etc..

Can people still make money with porn with all the free shit

available like the tube sites and torrents?

Yes, with rare exclusive specialized "real" no-bullshit content you can still do quite well. But you have to have lived the experience and everything needs to be authentic and not staged. People like real shit and I don't front them with my product. Reality porn has to be real in my opinion. My sites NDN Girls and Toticos are prime examples. Not all the girls are model perfect, but they are definitely the real deal.

Do your family and friends know about your porn business?

Yes they know, though I rarely discuss it because my life doesn't revolve around porn. I just consider it a fun lucrative hobby that I happen to be good at just because I've been doing it for so long. For me porn solves more problems than it creates so it's worthwhile for me. It's far better than just tricking off with girls. It's like a return on the initial investment the way I look at it.

Are you ever recognized in public?

Fruit stands, dollar stores, middle of the street, bus stations, yeah. Here and back in America unfortunately. Usually people I don't know running up to me giving me high fives and whatnot but it sometimes catches me off guard and niggas don't realize I don't like to talk about some porn episode on my site while I'm in line in the grocery store, but I guess its cool. I sometimes think I need to change my hat and/or not wear the same clothes I have on in the videos in public.

What's the best thing that ever happened at a porn shot you were on? What's the worst?

I'm happy anytime a girl swallows or takes a load on the face then smiles big afterward. The enthusiasm makes my day. It really makes my day. Some girls put their back into it, others are there to do the minimum amount of work possible. I prefer the ones that put some effort and love into the scene as it makes the end product better and me happier. The worst thing that's happened on shoots here: power outages, running out of tape/memory card space/battery packs, and uncooperative girls. If I get a girl that really doesn't want to be here and has no enthusiasm, I send her home and cut my losses. That has happened a few times. I think the main thing is to pick girls that really, really want to be in front of the camera that are mature enough to realize it's their life, their body, and their decision.

What's the best part of the DR? The worst?

The beaches, the warm weather, and the girls are the best part. They're all very affordable. The ones that aren't usually aren't worth your time anyway. Everyday is an adventure here. Life is much more exciting than anywhere else I've been. One thing for sure is you won't be bored here.

The worst part of DR is everyone hustles you or attempts to as a gringo. People pretend they don't have change when you buy stuff, street hustlers beg and extort, etc. There's a lot of traps and you can't get a straight deal in too many places as a gringo. Once you adapt to the gringo/expat lifestyle though you've got it made in the shade and learn to avoid all the pitfalls and live your life. The tourists fresh off the plane don't have a clue for the most part what they are in for, but if they're only here for a few days there's no need to bother learning anything. Just come, spend, and leave like it's Vegas.

Who is your favorite porn star of all time?

Other than myself, Misty Stone. She's my curly haired monster.

Favorite website?

Other than Toticos and NDN Girls I actually enjoy blog-style tourist websites like Trike Patrol, Black Vagina Finder, Habib Show, Filipina Sex Diary, Mr No Good anything with realism that's not staged with lots of humor thrown in the mix. In a way I consider the sites educational. I don't take any of this seriously and try to have fun with the girls and whatnot when I do movies. Some people say I laugh and joke too much and have too much fun. Also I like to see familiar places and faces that I can relate to.

What do you think about prostitution?

Define prostitution.

Cam Model AstroDomina aka Sydney Lee

AstroDomina is a Filipina cam model now based in the United States. The first time I encountered her, she was fully nude and humping a large stuffed animal in a public show. Sydney is attractive enough but she has something beyond that to draw in fans. I can't quite put my finger on what it is. Maybe this interview will help.

How and when did you get into webcamming?

I was in a desperate situation back then, not financially, but for a complete and utter change. "Webcamming" seemed to be the only option that doesn't involve having a boss, which is phenomenal, so I went for it.

What's your best sexual memory? What's your worst?

I have a couple of "best" sexual memories. Sex on top of Red Rock mountain, sex on the beach and a pool in Miami, and sex on a 747-Boeing plane. Hands down, best sexual memories ever! Worst? Being rammed by a 13 incher.

If you could start over again would you still have gotten into camming?

Probably not. Because it's very addicting! And once I pop, I can't stop!

If you had all the money you could ever want or need, would you have done camming?

If I had a lot of money, I wouldn't be on the computer 24/7 which is how I found out about camming. I'd be visiting the monks in Tibet, kangaroo spotting in Australia or scuba diving in Maldives.

What are the best and worst things that have come out of your camming experience? Has anything ever made you want to quit?

Camming is a great experience because you interact with people from all over the world at that very moment in time. No matter what timezone or country you are in, I come to you or you come to me. Easy as that. I create relationships with different individuals and learn a lot of things. Add to that, the feeling of being an internet celeb is always a plus. I don't have any particular worst moments, just when my cam score on MyFreeCams goes down. Haha.

You've branched into other things like pay per view video and a membership website. Which is your favorite? Which is the most lucrative?

Camming is still one of my favorites. However, pay per view video is starting to really grab my interest. I discovered that I enjoy creating custom clip videos for clients and I've been focusing on that lately. What's even more interesting, I created another account for my pay per view site called "Astro Dungeon" to focus on multi-fetish stuff. That's how much I like it! The membership program takes a lot of work. But if you analyze it well, it's definitely the most lucrative if I put a lot of eggs into the nest and wait for it to hatch every month.

You've said that you're in school for architecture. I think

that's awesome. Do you worry that your adult work may inhibit your ability to make it as an architect later?

Thank you! It's not an easy course. I don't plan on working for a firm. I plan on opening my own firm! I want to create houses or structures for anyone, even those in the adult business. Or maybe even design my own sex toys. Who knows? Sky is the limit. And if anyone judges me for my adult work and not my awesome creative abilities, it's their loss. I could have made them their dream house shaped like a dildo

I know you have videos for sale on MyFreeCams and Clips4Sale. Do you have any sexual content with men or is it all solo, fetish and girl/girl?

I have about 300 videos, some of which aren't really up for grabs because of really explicit content. However, I do film with men generally for fetish clips. I mostly have solo, fetish, and girl on girl videos.

Have you had any issues with family or friends finding out about your adult work? Has it caused any problems in your personal life?

My entire family knows that I cam. I know, shocker. I didn't intentionally tell them. My son-of-a-bitch ex did. Anyway, what's done is done right? Let bygones be bygones. No reason for me to call him a wanna-be politician imbecile who can't even satisfy my vagina with an 8 incher. But hey, sometimes I can't help it. Haha!

What would your advice be to a person wanting to follow in your footsteps? How about if it was a sister of yours? Would that change things?

My advice would be: "Follow your dreams. Don't let anyone,

even your own parents, get in the way".

Would you say the average cam girl more or less money over their career than they would have if they done a "vanilla" job (notice I said average and not a standout girl like you)?

When I cam, I put my best foot forward. I don't half-ass my way through my 3-hour session. I entertain like I have never entertained before. And when I do so, the money comes. Don't chase after the money, for you'll never catch it.

Do you watch porn? Who is your favorite porn star of all time?

YES! TERA PATRICK! But I haven't seen her in a while though.

What do you think of prostitution?

The oldest profession in the King James Bible.

What was your earliest sexual experience with a woman?

I can't remember exactly when but I can definitely say that I was already old enough to have a beer in a club!

Spit or swallow?

Spit if the cum tastes like acid. Swallow if its sweet. YES BOYS! Your diet affects the way your cum tastes! If your woman doesn't swallow, that means you gotta drink more water and eat healthier!

Have you ever met one of your cam fans? If so, how was it?

Yes I have. It's always so surreal. Meeting someone who watches you on a computer while you do sexually entertaining things? It's always surreal and a bit awkward. But at the same time, you feel like you gain a supporter; someone who is a real human being

What is your favorite book? Favorite movie?

Fave Book: "Rich Dad, Poor Dad." Favorite Movie: None.

If you were going out on your own for the day and not camming or planning to have sex, would you rather wear grannie panties, a thong or no panties at all?

I don't think they sell granny panties anymore... do they!? I haven't seen those in a while. However, I wear a drop-dead gorgeous silk lingerie or a hot pair of bra and panty set from Victoria's Secret. It's my secret to boost confidence.

How long do you plan on gracing the world with your awesome cam shows, videos and pictures?

I don't have an exact plan on how long I am going to cam (but why should I stop something I enjoy?). I definitely think I am going to continue making video clips since I am now an official clip producer (fancy name for a fancy job). My photo shoots are always fun and fabulous and I love creating images for different photographers, so no plan on stopping there as well. But one thing is for sure: I want world domination!

Any final words for my readers?

Ladies and gentlemen, sex is a great thing. Without sex, your relationship won't reach its ultimate potential. But make sure you graduate college first before you plan on doing a lot of sex. You'll have plenty of time after college guaranteed.

Porn Star Aurora Snow

Aurora Snow was a staple of the porn industry who came to my attention when she began writing thought provoking pieces for mainstream outlets. Luckily, she is quite accessible and was up for an interview.

I know you've been asked this many times, but it will help readers who are unaware: how and when did you get into porn?

I entered the adult business in May of 2000. I answered a newspaper ad for nude modeling and to my surprise things took off from there.

What's your best sexual memory? What's your worst?

Hmmm…. I don't know that I have sexual memories. I recall my interactions with partners more than the sex itself, unless the sex just happened yesterday, it's the feeling of it all that I recall the most – personally speaking. Are you asking about my best and worst moment on set at work?

If you could start over again would you still have made porn?

Probably. Being in adult has led me on an interesting journey. I am happy with where I have ended up. I entered the business a shy book smart kid in her first year of college. I am now a more social well rounded person with street smarts to accompany all of those books I read.

If you had all the money you could ever want or need, would you have done porn?

Honestly? No. I entered porn for the money. It was the only reason I got in. So obviously if I'd had all the money in the world, or even if I had parents that paid for my education I probably would not have entered porn. However that being as it is, I am not unhappy with myself and have very few regrets in life. No more regrets than your average person.

What are the best and worst things that have come out of your porn experience?

The worse things that have come from my porn career are the lousy ways its changed any relationship I have or may one day want. It's social baggage that no one can fathom when they first enter. The world doesn't think being a porn star is "cool" the way the entertainment industry does. It's eliminated some of my future career options and it's also lessened my credibility in some ways. No one believes girls who do porn are smart, or at least very few do.

However on the flip side of that I have been given more opportunities because of the business than I would have been given without it. I have worked with some of the top photographers, been in mainstream movies, and magazines and best of all granted an amazing opportunity to write for The Daily Beast. I'd always wanted to write ultimately and so in a way I am doing exactly what I've always wanted to do. And that is rare.

How long have you been writing? How did you start?

I have been an amateur writer most of my life. However I penned my first magazine column for an adult magazine five years ago and began writing for The Daily Beast in 2010.

Do you prefer writing or fucking on film?

I always make it a point to enjoy what I do whatever it is that I am doing.

Do you find that some outlets don't take your writing seriously because of your adult work?

That will always be a possibility. The real question is will anyone take me seriously if and when I want to write about a subject outside of sex or porn.?

Have you had any issues with family or friends finding out about your adult work? Has it caused any problems in your personal life?

Of course. It affects every relationship I've ever had. It's hard for people to understand.

What would your advice be to a person wanting to follow in your footsteps and start making porn? How about if it was a sister of yours? What that change things?

Maybe this makes me a hypocrite but if I had a sister I wouldn't want her to do porn. It's a tough business and very few girls are smart enough to save the money they make and go on to do something else. Most girls get wrapped up in the "lifestyle" don't bother to pay taxes, spend just as much as they make, and then when the work isn't as frequent they start working for less and less money just to keep working. After a certain amount of time the law of diminishing returns goes into effect. Some girls leave the business with less than they began because they leave in debt. There are a few that don't, but only a very few.

How do you think porn can continue to be profitable with

all of the free content now available online? Has the advent of file sharing, tube sites and the like put a big dent in your earnings?

It cannot be. That's the hard truth everyone is afraid of. There are less companies that shoot less and don't pay as much. Ten years ago porn was profitable, but now companies are struggling with how to profit and go forward long term.

Would you say the average porn star makes more or less money over their career than they would have if they done a "vanilla" job?

In the beginning of any girls career for the first 3 to maybe 5 years she'll make more than most but as the years go by the yearly income dwindles. Again, law of diminishing returns.

Who is your favorite porn star of all time?

Lauren Phoenix was always one of my favorites, Gauge, and Sunny Lane and

What do you think of prostitution?

I see nothing wrong with it. It's the oldest profession in the world. It shouldn't be illegal. It's a perfectly acceptable profession, its between consenting adults. One wants to buy something another is offering. Nothing wrong with that. I believe in free will. I don't believe in the pimp and control aspect that sometimes pops up, but perhaps if it were all legalized and not punishable by law then the pimp aspect would die out.

What do you think of bukkake? Japanese porn?

To each his/her own. I am not a fan but I know many that love bukkake. I've never done one because I just couldn't get into it. As for Japanese porn, I cannot say I have watched much of it.

Andrea Dworkin?

I think she only saw pornography one way. There are of course some violent aspects and that's what she focused on. She failed to focus on the positive aspects. Most people are either pro-porn or anti-porn. Very few are willing to say it can be both good and bad depending on what you are watching and how you deal with it personally. It's just like anything, food can even be both good and bad for you.

What is your favorite book? What book would you recommend to a porn fan who rarely reads?

Tough. I'm really loving "Going Clear" by Lawrence Wright. However I also just read "The Racketeer" by John Grisham, I read that book in about a day it was a quick read. I've read all of Stephen King and Michael Crichton's books. Kurt Vonnegut is also one of my favorite all time authors.

Have you ever done live stripping or webcamming? How was it?

Of course. Most girls in porn have. I am not much of a stripper, I just have fun on stage and give a show.

I kind enjoyed web camming a lot. If I'd known how much fun it could be I'd probably have begun doing it sooner. I have fun creating personalized shows for my web cam viewers.

How long do you plan on gracing the world with your awesome videos and pictures?

I have no idea. For as long as it makes sense I suppose.

Porn Producer Rick Nasty

Rick Nasty is a porn producer that puts out a lot of really authentic, home-grown looking content. I wanted to find out what made the guy tick.

When did you see your first porn?

I seen my first porn around maybe 11 or 12. I can't really remember, but I think it was around that age.

How did you get into porn? Were you involved in swinging before?

I got in the porn game around 2009, my uncle was supposed to start a company, but he didn't know exactly what he was doing, so I kinda just started filming stuff, and doing my own thing. I never been a swinger.

Can people still make money with porn with all the tube and download sites?

Hmm, this is a good question, and here is my answer: there is money to be made in the business, but people come in the business with the wrong idea and the wrong expectations. Please understand that the tube sites and all those other free sites do take away from the profit, but in some cases it helps to promote your material. Now the only way to survive in this business is to have more than one website.

People want more for their money, so you have to give them more. I have seen several people come into the business, with the best looking girls, good material, good marketing, good everything, and 6 months later, they are out the business, because they felt the money wasn't coming fast enough, or because people didn't respond the way they felt people should have.

Here is a secret to any porn site: you will know if your website is successful within the first 2 weeks. When something is good and has a market, it doesn't take people a long time to catch on to it.

How do you find models? Is it hard to find girls who will take multiple cocks on video?

This is a good question, haha. I wont give out all the secrets, but to be honest, this business and lifestyle is not for everyone. If it was, every guy that wants to do this would be doing it. I find girls all over, on the street on line, etc.. I even hand out cards, and I pulled a few good ones handing out the cards. No it isn't that hard to get them to take on 2 dudes at a time, haha.

Do your friends and family know what you do? Has your adult work ever caused you any problems in your personal life?

Yes, my family knows exactly what I do, and so do my close friends. My work hasn't really caused a problem in my personal life as of yet. But we will see.

What's the best thing that ever happened at a porn shot you were on? What's the worst?

Damn, so many good things have happened on set, its hard to pin point one thing. The worst thing has to be a guy I hired couldn't perform, and that shit was the worst, it almost made me want to get out the business, haha.

Who is your favorite porn star of all time?

Hmm, female performers: Kelly Star, Sky Black. Male performers : Wesley Pipes, Justin Slayer, and Devlin Weed.

What do you think about prostitution?

Well, I don't feel that it should be illegal. And it think its only illegal because it cant be taxed! I feel that what happens between two adults is their business, trading sex for money or other things goes on all the time. The real question is, whats the difference between porn and prostitution, but we will save that for another time.

Describe the perfect woman.

My perfect women is sexy, good personality, goal orientated, submissive but has her own mind, humorous respects herself as well as others. I am really into personalities.

You're from the Bronx right? What's the pay-for-sex scene like there? Are the street whores still working Hunts Point like they did in those HBO specials back in the day?

Haha, I am from Harlem homie. But the sex for pay scene is kinda dead, haha. They cleaned a lot of those areas up. Everything is on line, chat lines, and social networks etc..

Photographer Igor Smith

When does an interview with a photographer belong in a book like this? When the photographer takes lots of nude photographs that are very much unlike the usual stuff you find. Meet Igor Smith.

How did you get into photography?

My mom was a photographer in the 70s so I had cameras around all my life. In high school I took a class and started shooting punk bands and I never put a camera down again.

Do you prefer writing or taking photos?

By far photography, but I like to write about my photos as well. They say a photo is worth a thousand words so why not give 'em 2000.

When did you begin doing nude photography? How did you get into it?

I used to always shoot my girlfriends and stuff growing up and being the pervert I am it became a big part of my photography.

How, if at all, do you make money from your nude photography?

I shoot a lot of the naked stuff just as content for my website. I make ad revenue from my site but it's only about a fifth of my income. I do sell nude stuff from time to time and I just started doing a monthly feature for Hustler which pays pretty well and they give me a lot of freedom to do what I want instead of your standard pretty girl porn stuff.

Do you differentiate between nude photo shoots and "pornography"?

Personally I don't even like shooting spread leg stuff but I feel like the line for me is drawn at penetration.

What's the craziest experience you've had on a shoot?

I have a camera in my hand all the time, so all my craziest experiences turn into photo shoots. I will give you a weird sex one though because I know that's what you are looking for. I would never do this now that I am a pro, but when I first started shooting I photographed a friend of mine who was really nervous about shooting. She asked me to get naked if she was going to be naked. I told her I didn't want to get naked unless I was hard cause I think flaccid dicks look creepy. So the whole shoot, which ended up being like two hours, I was pretty much jerking off. She was masturbating as well and we both just got super horny and crazy but we never even touched each other. At the end I came on her tits and we took photos of that too but we never even kissed. It was pretty hot, but not exactly the most professional moment of my career.

What do you think about prostitution?

As long as the girl feels safe and is protected I am all for it. Personally I have never paid for sex, but sex has always come pretty easy for me and I haven't been in a situation where I needed, or wanted to pay for it. I have a ton of friends who escort and most of them seem pretty happy with it, but they are all high class girls who get references and charge a ton. I worry about the girls on the lower end. One of these days I will probably pay for it just for the experience of it, but I haven't yet.

Who is the hottest woman of all time in your opinion?

I was obsessed with Drew Barrymore as a kid and then I moved to Gina Gershon. These days I don't really have a favorite but fortunately I get to look at really hot girls all the time.

What is your favorite book?

I will say "Women" by Bukowski because that is an appropriately creepy answer.

What books, films, websites or other media would you recommend to people who like the work you do?

Late Night Feelings has a bunch of my favorite contemporary adult photographers working together and it's all free so I would start there. Most of my photographic influences aren't really of the naked variety but the obvious stuff would be like Terry Richardson and Richard Kern and then photographers who mix party photos with nudity like Last Nights Party or Kirill Was Here.

Where do you find your models?

At this point they find me. It used to just be my friends and girls I would meet at parties. I am pretty good at convincing people that getting naked for me for free is a good idea so it would just be random people I meet. A lot of people use Model Mayhem but I haven't really had good luck there. Twitter seems to be a pretty good way to meet models but you have to be at least a little bit established for that.

What advice do you have for guys or girls wanting to get into nude photography?

Photograph girls you know. Talk to friends and girlfriends and see if they would be interested. Tell them that you won't use the photos without their permission. Hopefully you get some shots you can both be proud of. NEVER fuck girls over and do anything with photos they don't want out there. I have a perfect reputation for keeping things secret so that people trust me and usually they will let me use photos they never thought they would let see the light of day. Once you have some decent images you can try sites like Model Mayhem or whatever and track down some more professional models. Don't be a scumbag and don't think you are going to make a living off of it. Do it for the images and people will want to work with you.

Porn Star Annie Cruz

Annie Cruz is a Filipina-American porn star. She did a lot of the usual stuff early on, which was good enough, but in my opinion she really began to stands out later on because of her unique personality and fetish performances.

Although you've surely been asked this before, could you remind my readers how and when you got into porn?

During my freshman year of college – a private Catholic university in northern California – I had an enormous sexual awakening, and although I watched A LOT of porn and was known for being quite the exhibitionist on campus, I never thought I would end up doing it. Sometime later, a couple of friends gave me a mini-intervention due to my sexual endeavors and after a counselor and my mother told me I had a sex problem (and to "fix it") – somehow, I ended up in porn during the beginning of my sophomore year of college. In Oct 2003, I shot my first scene, a girl/girl scene, for Asian Diva Girls, a company based in the bay area. From that point forward, I was in love with being in front of the camera, and it was then that my adventure eventually brought me to porn valley in Los Angeles.

What is your first sexual memory? What is your best?

My first sexual memory as in my earliest? I started masturbating at an incredibly young age, when I accidentally stumbled upon scrambled porn on an old television I had in my bedroom. As for my best memory...there are so many memories of which I cannot just choose one because different people, different circumstances, different everything all create a variation of great ones. However, I will give a fun one: The first time I ever squirted, when I was 18 years old. I had no idea what had happened after I gushed all over this guy, and it was a year following that, did I understand and start to learn the art of female ejaculation.

What is the most taboo sexual thing you did before you got into porn?

It all depends on what is even considered taboo anymore. I suppose I could say pegging – the act of female to male strap-on anal sex – would be one thing. During my sophomore year of college, my best friend at the time had wanted to fuck me anally, and I told him I would let him if he would allow me to fuck him in the ass first. He let me, and as agreed, I let him return the favor. I also learned what it was like to be in a D/s (Dominant/submissive) relationship, when I was 18, in addition to playing with light bondage and pain play.

Did you ever get into swinging, dogging, group sex or anything else out of the "norm" before you did porn?

I was in a living relationship with another woman before I moved to LA from San Francisco to pursue porn full-time. We would often prey on unsuspecting men, bring them back to our place, fuck them, and then kick them out because we rarely shared our bed with anyone other than each other over night. Sometimes, we would go to a sex club in San Francisco and let people watch us, and there was one time, when we brought one guy with us, who was unable to "perform." I have a fond memory in which we invited a guy over, left him in the bedroom, so that we could take a bath and have sex, while he sat waiting. There were more than just threesomes too, and of course, we also shared other women together. I loved her because she was so open-minded and uninhibited like myself, and for the record, the only woman I could submit to. Dogging – public sex – was something I often did as well. Bar bathrooms. Parks. Parties. Playgrounds. Convent patio of the Catholic college I went. Against a tree in the woods. The list goes on...

Aside from the threesomes and foursomes I indulged in pre-porn, I did my first gangbang, when I was a freshman in college. 5 guys. They tag-teamed me anally, and I also did my first DP (double penetration). It wasn't until I met ex-husband during my first year in porn that I discovered the swinging lifestyle, swing parties, and having an open relationship.

If you could start over again would you still have done porn?

I have grown a lot, learned a lot and done so much because of porn. It's been one interesting roller coaster ride that has given me opportunities to do music videos, mainstream movies, magazines, etc. Not to say I needed porn to do these things, but still, I am grateful for a lot of wonderful things that I have been lucky to do. I don't have any regrets, so I don't know if I could say that I wouldn't have done it if I could start over. There are plenty of things I'd have done differently in the beginning, sure. I suppose had I not gone down that road, I'd have pursued mainstream Hollywood instead. I took drama in high school and have always loved acting.

If you had been born with all the money you could ever want or need, would you have still done it?

Honestly, when I first started in this business ten years ago, I used to joke with people that if I was a millionaire, I'd still do porn because of how much I love it. There were so many times throughout my years in porn that I often told myself, "Wow, I almost forgot I'm getting paid to do this." If I was born with all the money I wanted, I probably would have done it just for kicks, not in a career-driven way but rather just for fun – do a few scenes just to say I did or to fulfill some fantasies I may have.

Have you had any issues with family or friends finding out about your adult work? Has it caused any problems in your personal life?

My maternal grandmother was the first of my entire family to address the truth about my doing porn. She said to me, "You're my granddaughter. I love you. Nothing will ever change the fact that you are my granddaughter." My parents soon accepted it, and they – along with the rest of my family – fully support me.

Do you have any fetishes?

Who doesn't? ;) I particularly love feet. I love having my feet kissed and sucked, while I am having sex. It drives me wild. I also love doing the same for others as well. For a really long time, I had a thing for hands. You don't hear that too often, right? Then again, there's a fetish for EVERYTHING. There's also something very naughty about watersports that I love. And of course, I'm into BDSM, and I love Dominating worthless fools and helpless submissives.

You seem to do more around watersports and squirting than a lot of other women in porn. Is that because you like it, because fans like it, or some combination of both?

I love it! And so there's no confusion for anyone reading this, watersports and squirting are two different things – although, both happen to be very wet. Ten years ago, I wouldn't be saying I'm into pee play, but after having a bunch of girls pee on me once for a film, it changed my perspective on the fetish. I also love peeing on people who love it. As for squirting, I absolutely get thrilled, when I am able to make a woman, who has never squirted before, squirt. Female ejaculation is something that many people are still skeptical about, and while there are many, who may just be suffering from coital incontinence rather than actually orgasming or ejaculating, it really does exist. It's a different sensation and feeling, and you can definitely tell the difference between "squirt" and urine. It's all in the taste and/or smell.

What is the most embarrassing thing that happened to you in adult work? Is there any content out there that you wish you could make disappear?

There aren't so much embarrassing things but rather a choice I made that I wish I had not. I did a movie for Anabolic (a double anal scene) in which the director thought it would be funny for me to tell a fictitious story about losing my anal virginity at a young age, so I said that I lost it to my stepfather to over-dramatize the story. I don't even have a stepfather in real life, hence why I said it. Since it was all an act, I didn't think much of it; I didn't think about the repercussions of saying such a thing. That particular movie haunts me to this day with fans and people questioning me and pitying me, when it was all just fiction. When I have to explain myself, lots of people tend to disbelieve me. So, I'll say it here now for the record: I do not have a stepfather (never have) nor was I raped anally at a young age. In fact, the first time I ever had anal sex was during my freshman year of college, and it was consensual. When it comes down to it, the only thing that matters is that I know the truth, and people, who know me personally, can attest that I am somewhat of a twisted fuck, who obviously made the wrong decision in creating a sick story for a film. It was a silly porn, people; not art imitating life. Do you question Tom Hanks for being gay and having AIDS just because of the movie Philadelphia? Moving on…

How is it shooting with Kink?

For the longest time, Kink was once my favorite company to shoot for. They always took care of the models and work with everyone's comfort levels. Also, contrary to what many may believe, their stuff looks a lot scarier than it really is.

What do you think of sites like Facial Abuse?

Frankly, I'm personally not into the sort of things sites like that produce. "Why did you shoot for them?" Some may ask. Well, I didn't go through some of the emotional breakdowns or regrets that one would imagine most women, who have shot for sites like FA, would. I'm pretty fucking tough, and sometimes, it's fun to see how far I can take it. But still, I am sure many are still questioning why I did it. I have a really interesting story about my experience shooting for them. James Deen was my scene partner, and we had done numerous scenes together prior to working together for FA. The producers were bragging about how girls can't handle their scenes with them, and how no one can ever be too extreme for that company. Challenge accepted. James and I laughed at them, and I looked at him and said, "Only one rule, James: Don't punch me in the nose." We did an incredibly rough scene – the roughest scene Deen claims he has ever done if you just ask him. Our scene was so extreme that the director made us do a verbal consensual confirmation on camera afterward. By the time the scene hit the internet, there was so much unusable footage too hardcore for them that the scene was cut down to 16 minutes. And I assure you, our scene was much longer than 16 minutes. Challenge completed. Would I ever shoot for them again? No, I already did it once just to do it. Would I recommend other girls to shoot for them? No. Unless you truly are into that sort of "abuse," by all means go for it. I don't knock people's fetishes or desires, and there are some, who are really into that sort of thing.

How much of what you say is acting and how much is a genuine love of sex? I remember seeing you on an episode of Howard Stern riding a Sybian and you said you loved sex and would fuck random guys on the street. Do you really do that? I know an American girl who is into finding random guys to fuck but she says she actually has a lot of trouble finding safe, willing partners online or elsewhere. Any advice for her and others in her position?

The reason why I got into porn in the first place is because of my genuine love for sex (just see my answer to question 1). Back in 2006, when I first appeared on Stern's show, I probably would have fucked randoms. Times change, however, and so do I. Don't misunderstand – many can affirm I still have my insatiable appetite for sex; I am just much pickier about the partners I choose and where I find them, especially since people in the adult biz have the trust to keep each other safe by being safe outside of "work." Before I got into porn, I frequently found my random partners from the internet (obviously, I stopped doing that ages ago) or from places I just went to. I was always extremely forward, so perhaps that is why it was so easy for me to meet people. I remember a time, walking in downtown San Francisco with my ex-gf, and as we walked past a good-looking guy, I simply started talking to him. Flirting. Next thing I know, I'm at his place. A lot of people act like it's difficult. It really isn't. If your friend has problems finding willing partners online, where is she looking? I suppose the best advice I can give her is to join a website that specializes in adult meetings (like Adult Friend Finder for example) if she hasn't already tried that. It seems to be a much better bet compared to my wary encounters from random chat rooms back in the AOL and yahoo days.

How do you think porn can continue to be profitable with all of the free content now available online? Has the advent of file sharing, tube sites and the like put a big dent in your

earnings personally?

It's tough to say. I started in this business in late 2003, and it's incredible how much of it has changed over the years. Back then, it was extremely profitable. These days, companies have diminished, while some shoot less now and don't pay as much. Both producers and performers are constantly struggling. Surprisingly, I still get sign-ups to my website (though not as nearly as much as I used to years ago), but it's not much. Would it change if I started generating traffic again? I don't know. Things are just too different now. However, my current income comes mostly from wrestling these days as I don't really shoot porn anymore.

Who is your favorite porn star of all time?

It's hard to choose just one. I have nothing but a lot of love and respect for Ginger Lynn and Nina Hartley – these are true Porn Stars from their time and even now. Porn has evolved so much throughout the years, and I feel like I should have done porn in another era...back when women truly loved sex and expressing it. Unfortunately, over the years, women like that are hard to come by. I also mustn't leave out Belladonna, who wasn't afraid to do what she wanted or how. Lastly, I have much respect for Tera Patrick. Aside from being gorgeous and smart, she defied the stereotypes most people have of women in porn.

What do you think of bukkake? How about Japanese porn?

In all of the crazy things I have done in porn and out, I have never done a bukkake. I feel like I would have to be in a very submissive and humiliating position to endure that, and it's quite difficult to put me in a submissive position. I've never really watched Japanese porn, but hentai on the other hand, makes for great masturbatory material.

What do you think of prostitution? Would you ever consider escorting?

Personally, escorting isn't my cup of tea. It just isn't something that interests me, so I don't think I'd ever consider doing it. In porn, performers are required to have a clean test to shoot, and they know who their partners are. To me, that was much safer because of the trust everyone has amongst each other. I used to have a very strong opinion on escorting (I was totally against it), but I realized in the end, we are all whores in our own little ways after all whether or not in the sex industry, haha. My biggest concern for those, who escort, is safety and protection – sexually and otherwise.

I know you're Filipina, but I've read that you were born in America. How connected are you with the Philippines? Do you visit often? What do you think of the huge prostitution scene there, especially the huge commercial districts like Angeles City?

I have only visited the Philippines once, and I was 3 years old. I am not really that connected with the PI, so I couldn't tell you how I feel about the prostitution scene out there. However, off topic – my mother has told me many times that the hookers out there are absolutely stunning, especially the ladyboys.

Do you do feature dancing, adult webcamming and things along those lines? Do they pay better than porn shoots? Are they fun or a pain in the ass?

I have considered feature dancing. Webcamming is fun, but it's also exhausting because my most frequent request is squirting. A girl can fake an orgasm, but squirting is an entirely different thing. I found that doing that continuously for a long period of time fatigued me brutally in addition to fans being super demanding. I always try to do different things to mix it up like anal and DP, so doing all of that plus squirting sometimes didn't

69

seem to be enough. Camming can be great money but definitely not more than what one would make on a porn shoot in a day.

Ever run into any weird or creepy fans that caused problems?

Yes, many times on several occasions, and I'd rather not give them the pleasure by discussing it/them here publicly

How long do you plan on gracing the world with your amazing videos and pictures?

I've been pursuing other projects outside of porn as of late. Not to say that one cannot find me in other videos and photos that are not porn-related, however. In which case, I'll grace the world until someone tells me I shouldn't anymore, haha. Aside from smut that can be found on my website, which I plan to keep up until I feel it's time to shut down, I'll always have wrestling. Pro-wrestling fans can enjoy my alter ego Nasty Annie Gunn at Pro Style Fantasies.

What advice do you have for other women who are considering getting into porn?

The porn world has changed drastically these past few years. With piracy and tube sites continuing to kill the industry, I don't feel like it's a smart move to start in a business that feels like it's feast or famine for plenty of others. I would not recommend anyone to pursue work in porn right now. However, if this is truly something one wants to get into, be sure of the following:

Understand the repercussions of working in adult. If you don't want friends or family knowing, there is a huge chance, they will know sooner or later.

Only do it if you enjoy sex…and understand that porn sex is different than "home sex"

Don't ever let anyone control what you want or don't want to do. You are the only, who can decide this.

Know that if you plan to get another job after having done porn for a long period, it may be difficult

Don't just do it for the money; as previously stated, the biz has extremely changed with companies shooting less and paying less. Girls are working for half their rates just to make ends meet or to keep working, and it's sad.

What was the last book you read?

"Batman Earth One" by Geoff Johns is the last graphic novel I read. I am currently reading "The Stranger Beside Me" by Ann Rule, the story of serial killer Ted Bundy

What are your plans for the future?

Right now, I am working on some comic book-related stuff that I'll announce more details with in the near future. I will continue to model, creating interesting and fascinating artistic pieces as seen in my non-porn mainstream portfolio. Film projects and the like are on my list of ventures currently. I'll still be creating websites for other people as I indulge in web/graphic design, when I have the time. I'd love to go back to school to study computer animation and/or game design. Lastly, I'm going to continue my travels all over the world and continue this crazy adventure I call my life.

To wrap up, thanks a lot for taking the time to answer these questions.

Thanks for having me!

Japanese Blow Job Bar Worker

And now to the cream on top. Sorry for the bad pun, but what is a more fitting introduction for an interview with a woman who performs oral sex to strangers day-in and day-out to make a living? That's what we have here. This interview was done via a public forum, with questions coming from anyone willing to ask them at at the time.

So just what is a pinsaro?

It is a shop where we give you a blow job. But we also do most things apart from full sex as well.

I see. How much and how long?

Our shop charges shy of 6,000 Yen (60 dollars) for 30 minutes. Cheap places are about 2,000 (20 dollars).

So how much do you get of that?

2,000 Yen an hour, plus 1,000 for each blow job we do.

That's pretty low!

Give us your stats.

OK.

Sex: Female

Age: 22

Occupation: Student

Location: Kanto

Height: 160

Weight: 50

Measurements: 87 cm, ?, ?

Bra size: E

Boyfriend: Yes

How many guys dated: 6

Virgin: No

First time/place you had sex: 21 in the winter, at his house

How did you feel: "Finally!"

Number of sexual partners: 1

So how many do you do in a working day?

I do about 10 in a 7 hour shift. The most I ever did was 15 in 8 hours. I couldn't get the biggest in my mouth, because it was too thick and my jaw hurt.

Your first was at 21 and at 22 you work in a pinsaro? What happened?

I was working at it when I was a virgin.

Since you were a virgin, did they finger you?

It hurt a bit but I got through OK, if barely.

Do you wipe yourself down with anti-bacterial material after each customer?

I wipe myself. There's a special anti-bacterial cloth for it.

Does your jaw get sore?

It hurts if I keep doing a big person.

Do you do "*oyajikaeshi*"? [Being licked by a succession of customers one after another]

No. Honestly, I just want to wipe myself whenever they lick me.

How is the taste of penis?

Dull. Cum is salty though.

Tell us the name you use.

No way!

You were a virgin but worked at a pinsaro? Why?

I needed money and I was totally desperate.

Is it fun work?

It's no different to any other part-time work.

Do you get along with the other girls?

Yes, it's really lively in our waiting area!

Do you get a lot of old guys?

Lots of guys in their thirties and forties. We get customers aged

20 to 70 though.

Does your boyfriend know?

He doesn't know.

Do you have partitions between the booths? I want to go but I'm fat, am uncircumcised and am really small so I'm a bit hesitant.

It's like an internet cafe. There are no doors though. If you are clean there is nothing to worry about.

How much do you make a month?

150,000 – 200,000 Yen.

Do people proposition you for more outside the shop?

They do, but I decline them.

Do you mind if I spend all the time fondling your boobs?

Sure, I won't mind, in fact I'd be obliged to. But if all you want to do is fondle them then you can get it cheaper at a sex cabaret club.

Do you get guys with stinky, dirty penises?

There are some guys with spicy smelling penises. Luckily you can use your fingers.

So you can touch breasts at a pinsaro?

Sure. You can touch pussy too.

How do you clean your mouth? What about eating?

There is isodine mouthwash and tooth brushes. I don't eat as much.

What do you wear at work?

A school uniform. Like from high school. I take off as much as asked. Often customers prefer I just wear the skirt.

Do you swallow?

No. I have done it accidentally though, but refuse if asked.

You ever had full sex whilst working?

It's impossible. But I have come close. Because there are guys doing rounds in the place.

You really don't? I had a girl just mount me at one place, the guy didn't even take any notice.

That shop's funny. The shop could be shut down and the employees busted.

Can you titty fuck a girl at a pinsaro?

You can. I'm a bit too flat and there's no lube so I'm not very good...

Can you do 69?

Yes.

Will I be blacklisted for burying my face in your breasts for 30 minutes?

No, but I recommend an "oppai pub" [tit bar] or sex cabaret for that instead.

How much have you made since working at the pinsaro?

1,000,000 Yen working on and off.

Do you think you can get AIDS through unprotected fellatio?

Definitely. It's scary.

Does your shop use condoms or not?

No. If you prefer, we can.

Do you get foreigners? Are they really that huge?

We don't allow foreigners in. There are some really amazing Japanese out there though.

Don't you think this is unfair to your boyfriend?

I don't wish to discriminate against prostitutes – I think it's a splendid trade – but hiding that from the boyfriend you're dating is just despicable. It's worse than cheating.

If my girlfriend cheated on me I might be able to forgive her. But if she turned out to have been working as a prostitute I'd go crazy. I might even kill myself.

I think it's bad. I think it's despicable. I cannot excuse myself at all.

Have you ever been cheated on?

No. Although I'm sort of cheating on my boyfriend now, aren't I?

As a woman, do you regard men who visit brothels with contempt?

I work there, and I don't. Besides, doesn't every man visit a brothel at least once?

Lately I've been wondering if I should split with my girlfriend and just go to prostitutes instead.

Why not just go to a brothel whilst you have your girlfriend? Is there something wrong with that?

Porn Star Lucky Starr

Lucky Starr is an Asian-American porn star with an interesting background. As she explains below she came into her own doing MILF scenes. I first noticed her many years ago and spent significant time reviewing her own work for my own non-professional purposes.. I was more than happy to interview her.

How old are you and where are you from?

I'm 40 (41 at the end of the month), from Chicago, IL.

When and how did you get into porn?

I was waiting on tables and trying to get into mainstream acting, then I went to work one day and I was taken off the schedule. I was laid off and devastated. I was engaged to another man at the time, and asked how he'd feel if I started doing porn. He was all for it at the time. So I emailed pictures to Jim South, and the rest as they say is history. I'm not with the fiance' anymore. But I took my career and ran with it.

What was your first sexual experience?

Hmmm.. I started giving blow jobs at the age of 13. My boyfriend at the time was much older, he was 16. But I was kinda the blowjob queen in high school because I thought sex was sacred and didn't want to try it unless I was in love. And I was in love. I had sex with my high school sweetheart of 2 years. He's a doctor now, and married with 2 kids.

What was the first porn you watched?

The very first one I ever watched was the one with Sylvester Stallone before he became a star. It wasn't even really a porn, it was just weird 70s drug taking bullshit. But then I discovered such starlets as Ginger Lynn, and Amber Lynn, etc. And they're totally my buddies now!

How have your impressions of porn changed since you entered the industry?

Absolutely!! Porn used to really turn me on, but now I know so much about the industry and every aspect of how it works that it's nothing new to me now. My thing now is watching porn features just for the acting. There's actually some excellent ones out there.

With all of the free content around today, how do production companies continue to make money and pay models? Does commercial porn have a future?

Free content has hurt our industry significantly. I mean why pay for it, when you can get it for free? Since the tube sites, smaller companies have disappeared, the companies that have survived are paying less, so many porn girls have turned to other sources of income. There will always be a market for commercial porn. May not be as big or glamorous as before, but it will always exist.

What would you say to women who want to get into porn now?

Don't be shy, and be confident in your looks, body and sexuality. The main reasons people work are their look and their attitude. If you show up late, hungover, high on drugs, and covered in bruises, you probably won't work for that company again.

Have you or would you do any "outside" adult work like feature dancing, adult webcam modeling or escorting?

I would feature dance is given the opportunity, I have done some webcam work, but you only make money if someone buys a private show, so sometimes you can sit there for hours before someone takes the bait. And escorting.. well, let's just say that's a sensitive subject most of the ladies of the industry don't like to discuss, so I'll just leave that topic alone.

What do you think of prostitution?

I, personally, don't have a problem with prostitution. If two consenting adults want to do something that mutually benefits both parties, then who am I to judge?

What was your best experience in the adult industry? What was your worst?

My best was when I did the romantic feature where I won my award. The movie was "A Mother's Love 2" by Hard Candy Films. I put my heart and soul into that movie, and I wound up winning the XBIZ Award this year for Best Scene in a Couples Themed Feature. I cuddle with that trophy at night!

My worst was when I shot for a company called Facial Abuse. Don't get me wrong, I was grateful for the work, but there must have been a better way to get the point across without actually hitting me in the face full force. My throat started bleeding from the deep throating, I vomited several times, and for days afterwards I had bruises on my face. I couldn't eat solid food for days. It was all an act for the camera, I just wish there was a slightly gentler way to get the point across.

What do you think about condom requirements in porn?

I believe in the option to use condoms in porn, if it makes you feel better. Personally, I start getting yeast infections when exposed to condoms for a long time. Valid STD tests work for me. I don't prefer watching a porn with condoms.

You are often billed as a MILF in your videos. I don't know what it is but something about you is so hot. It's not that you're a "MILF." What do you think it is?

It's my age. They look at the numbers and immediately put me in a certain category.

What was your craziest sexual experience outside of the adult industry?

I used to go to swingers clubs with my ex. We weren't true swingers, but he liked to watch me with other men. After awhile, it seemed like a sex pit where people just seemed to jump in.

Have you had any problems with family or friends over your adult work?

Most of my friends are supportive. My only family that knows is my cousin that lives here in CA, and my sister. And I did NOT tell my sister. She found out on her own. The way she let me know was she sent me a present for my birthday last year that was a personalized item. The name was not my real name it was my stage name. Then I called her up and we talked about it.

When will you leave porn? What are your plans after you finish doing adult work?

I'll leave porn when I wake up one morning and say, "OK, I'm done with that." Been there, done that, got the tee shirt. After adult work, I'd like to do more mainstream acting.

Where can fans find out more about you? What would you like to say those reading this interview?

You can find out about my WHOLE LIFE on my blog which is luckystarr1.livejournal.com. It's a no holds barred look at my life and the adult industry. According to a lot of people, it's an amazing read! Also to those reading this interview, the best way to follow what I'm doing is my twitter @ClubLuckyStarr. I have a Facebook, but ONLY accept friend requests from people I know personally. But anyone can like my page!!

Porn Star and Cam Model Little Mina

Little Mina started out as a webcam model but has since transformed into something of a porn magnet. She runs her own little empire that includes videos of her and friends doing everything from fetish work to bareback gangbangs. I knew of her before I started my website but remained nothing more than a viewer until I finally reached out to do the following interview.

Give us some background about you.

My name is Mina Li. I am 4'9″ and I am the youngest and only daughter. I grew up with two older brothers. I love video games. Mainly first person shooting games. I own the PS4 and Xbox one.

What are your hobbies?

My hobbies are mainly relaxing, eating and playing video games.

What three websites do you check most often?

Twitter, Myfreecams, and Google.

Are you single?

Yes I am. And I'm not looking.

What was your first sexual experience?

The guy left me the next day after taking my virginity. He broke it off with me. But the sex was awkward. Since I was only 17.

What kind of sex do you like to have in your "normal life"?

I am not big on foreplay. I like to jump into blow jobs then fucking. I am a quickie kind of girl so I can relax and go right back at it. Haha.

How did you get into adult web camming?

Someone who was in the camming business for 2 years told me about it. So I thought is try it out and it's awesome.

How did that progress into making adult videos?

I was already making adult videos, haha. So why not make a little profit out of it. So I continued what I already have started, haha.

What's the story with the bukkake video you did? Was that your first bukkake?

My first bukkake was only jerking off 9-12 guys. It was awkward since there was random talking while I was trying to dirty talk or jerk them off, haha. The one I did with another model we only ended up with only 5 fans. But it turned our awesome. I had a guy who flew from Miami to attend this even which made me feel honored. I wanted to do something special for my fans to be part of my video.

What do your family and friends think about your adult work? Do they know?

My grandma lives with me. She thinks I'm taking pictures and everyone of my family members thinks I am a 'web designer' but I did go to school for web design so it's not too scratchy. Just until they ask to see my site then there will be a little problem. Haha.

You gained a bit of fame online for the video of you almost getting caught at work dildoing yourself. What's the story behind that?

It was my last day of work so why not go out with a BIG BANG, haha. Plus he can't fire me anyways. Haha so I decided to give a show. But I didn't think my last day was going to go viral. Haha. I'm not upset I did it

How did you feel when it started spreading around?

It got annoying when people kept asking if I was that one girl who almost got caught at work. But I'm glad the person who recorded it did it. Thanks to him it helped me boost my followers.

What kind of panties do you wear on a normal day?

Anything that fits, haha. Or sometimes nothing at all. Clothes are overrated.

What do you think about the tube sites? Do they hurt your income substantially?

They do. I'm not a big fan. But free porn is always a plus. I watch hentai so I can't complain too much.

What's the best thing about doing adult work? And what's the worst?

The best thing is I don't get to do so much. Just pleasure myself and others. Sometimes traveling sucks for me. I hate flying for hours and sitting in the car for hours. We need to invent teleportation. Better to travel. Haha.

What was your worst experience in this business so far?

Hmmm I guess it's when you just have those horrible days. Or when you forget something or if you have an appointment and they cancel at the last minute sucks.

Have you ever raffled off dates like so many models on MFC? If so how did it turn out?

I have never before until now. Not a big fan to raffle dates. I think everyone deserves a date of they really want it.

What do you think about escorting and erotic massage parlors?

I don't escort but if you do then go for it. I don't judge you on how you make a living. I judge you based on your personality. The erotic massage parlors, I don't know. Never been to one but hey if they offer I can't pass it off. Haha. A good extra way to release stress.

If you had a family member or friend who wanted to follow in your footsteps, what advice would you give them?

I actually have a cousin who wants to but at the moment she's not serious. The only advice I would give is if you are serious I will help you but if you want to goof around and party then this may have to wait until you are done partying. There's nothing wrong with partying but when you choose going clubbing than giving your guys a show they worked hard to get to, it looks bad on your part. But there are girls who are not serious about this and there are girls who do and it shows who are serious. But most important is one step at a time and have fun doing it.

What do you have planned for the future, both in the near and far terms?

I would love to own my own production company. And I know I'll get there.

Where can interested readers find you? What websites and projects are you involved in?

I'm always on twitter @little_mina69 my email is always available little_mina@live.com

The Guy Behind the Tuk Tuk Patrol Thai Porn Site

Tuk Tuk Patrol is a porn website that features Thai ladies not seen elsewhere. The premise is that white guys riding tuk tuks (which are motorcycle powered rickshaws used in Southeast Asia) pick up amateurs from the streets.

This interview was long in the making. I first reached out to people working with Tuk Tuk Patrol when my website went online. It took nearly a year to finally put this question and answer session together but I think the results show that the effort was worthwhile.

How and when did you get into porn?

Just on a whim one day about 8 years ago. Always loved porn so figured why not get into it myself? Do what I love. It started out just as a joking half-crazy idea for fun, but then I got more and more involved in it as I went.

Do you shoot in Asia because it's cheaper, more fun or for some other reason?

Mainly because it's where I am most comfortable and familiar. I've been coming to Asia for 15 plus years so it's really a second home for me. I really prefer being in Asia more than anyplace else. It's nice to go back home or visit other places once in a while, but I always end up missing Asia sooner than later. There's a certain feeling to being in Asia that's unlike being anywhere else and is hard to describe.

Is the kind of Asian content you do now what you started out with?

Yes.

When did you first travel to Asia? How did you find about the commercial sex scene there?

I had already of course heard the typical stories and seen the characterizations of it on TV and in movies and the like, but that all seemed so unreal; as if it was some mystical fairy tale Then when I first arrived, it was even more incredible than I had ever imagined or thought truly possible. I was amazed at just how "normal" it was here as compared to the West. It was truly another world.

How has the country changed since your first visit?

Thailand has changed in some ways, yes. Things like traffic, prices, etc....but overall, in the grand scheme of things, it's quite the same. Sure, the names of the playgrounds and players change, but the game really does stay the same. I think what happens a lot of times when you hear people pine for the "good ol' days" and lament about how things were so much better, in anyplace, it's more often than not a matter of THEM changing more than anything.

Have you been to any other countries known for their sex industries (like say, Costa Rica)? How did you like them?

Yes, I've been to the Philippines, Cambodia and the Dominican Republic. They all had their own pluses and minuses, but for me, Thailand still offers the most.

What is your first sexual memory? What is your best?

My first sexual memory was screwing a friend's aunt in his house when I was 17. Now, his aunt was the same age as us, oddly enough. She was your classic white blonde babe with big tits. At that time I never imagined becoming crazy about Asians; they actually didn't look appealing to me at all back then. My best sexual memory? Hmm, what (who) did I do last night? It all runs together but I've surely had some great ones.

What was the first porn you saw?

On VHS at my childhood neighborhood friends house while his parents were out at church on a Sunday morning: Double Wong Dong, starring Don Fernando and Cumisha Amado if I recall correctly.

What is the biggest inconvenience of making your porn flicks?

Inconvenience? Hmmm, not sure there is one for me really.

If you could start over again would you still have done porn? Do the benefits outweigh the costs?

For me, yes. Just because it's what I enjoy and I still enjoy it. It's all about what you want in life. I love the independence it's brought me. Working for the Man for 50 yrs to get a gold watch and pension at the end? No thanks.

Have you had any issues with family or friends finding out about your adult work? Has it caused any problems in your personal life?

No major issues. I'm fairly disconnected from the "real world" back home, so unless that could be called a major issue, no.

How difficult is it to find models? Is it more difficult now than it used to be? Some producers say the prices women want to model are rising and the amount they can actually make from the shoots are falling to the point where it almost doesn't make sense to even make porn anymore. What do you say about that?

In anything, you have to adapt to change. I've managed to do that quite well over the years and really don't have a major problem finding talent. Some of what your describing probably pertains to producers in the West, but here in Asia it's still profitable.

Are most of the girls you shoot with pro prostitutes, semi-pros or total amateurs? Have any run into problems after being in your movies?

I don't like to use labels, but I'd say most of the girls I shoot are amateurs. Sometimes you'll have one who regrets doing it later, especially once her content is online and she hears about it from someone. They'll have this weird "I'm so surprised" act, like they forgot they did it or never expected to see or hear about it. We all make choices in our lives we have to live with one way or another.

Have you ever had a model who smelled so bad down below that you've canceled a shoot?

Not canceled, but I've had a few stink-pots.

I've read that some guys who shot in Thailand but didn't hide their identities have actually been banned from reentering the country. What do you think about that?

I've read a lot about a lot of things. Some of which were true, some of which were only partly-true, and some of which were complete hogwash. There's a lot of people out there who never want to let the facts get in the way of a good story.

What do you think about prostitution and pornography in general?

To break it down in simpler terms, I think sex is part of life, quite literally. It's one of the most basic and natural human instincts. Trying to suppress it—-with religion, law, etc—is ultimately, a fool's errand. Both things, prostitution and porn, have been part of the human story since the dawn of man and will be until the end. There were displays of porn in every prehistoric society and ancient civilization. Hannibal had to slow his march through the Alps so the whores could keep up.

How do you think porn can continue to be profitable with all of the free content now available online? Has the advent of file sharing, tube sites and the like put a big dent in your earnings?

To some, in more generic niches, yes. The tubes and whatnot have hurt. But for us, it's actually been the opposite. Our profits continue to rise, almost inexplicably so. I think what we are seeing, is that people want something different. Something unique and specific. How many videos of Sara Jay or Jayden James taking a load to the face do we need to see? People still appreciate exclusive, originally themed content that they don't see 100 other places. I think that is what we provide and the growing membership numbers seem to support it.

Any problems with sexually transmitted infections after shoots?

No.

What do you think of Filipina and Thai porn stars that have become popular in America like Lana Croft, Annie Cruz, Priva and others?

God bless them. But again, I go back to my reply earlier. How many times do we need to see them? When it becomes about "the star" it loses something. It's about the sex and the excitement of sex. What's exciting about the same girl over and over again? Ask any married guy and you'll have your answer. That being said, I've surely fapped to most of those girls myself a few times.

How long do you plan on making porn?

As long as I still enjoy doing it.

What advice do you have for other guys who want to follow in your footsteps, not necessarily in Asia but in general?

In general, I would say: Do it for the love of doing it, or don't do it at all. If you're only in it for the money, the product will probably be lacking and you'll likely end up disappointed. The best things in the World come from those who put a real love and care behind it.

Any last words to readers?

Man who walk sideways through airport turnstile, always going to..........Bangkok!

Retired Japanese Porn Star

The following interview is a translation of a question and answer session that first appeared on the notorious 2Chan website in Japan.

A Japanese women who used to work in the local porn or "AV" industry made herself available to the website's anonymous users. That resulted in the impromptu interview that follows.

Can you give us your name, age, hometown and a pic of your face?

If I give you that, my life, already over at the best of times, will be even more over. Give me a break?

How did your friends react?

Variously. Some people didn't care and went on being my friend, but others were busy spreading rumors. One guy had all my DVDs, I was a rather perturbed by that.

Prove you're not a fake and upload a pic of your legs.

After retiring I spent years as a *hikikomori* NEET, so I look pretty different. So my legs are now just "pizza."

By the way, I was 18-19 when I was performing.

Did it feel good?

That really depends on the actor. Sometimes you cum normally, other times you need to act it up.

The notion that "porn actors = good" is nothing more than fiction. I think the old guys on set are more skilled.

Also, women who are having a good time really don't start squealing "an-an" like in an AV.

How much did you get paid?

I was getting about 500,000 ¥ ($5000 US Dollars) per AV. However, it changes a bit depending on the content. A shoot for a magazine would be a few tens of thousand Yen. Some people appearing in the films were actually intent on building connections – for an unsocial type like me it was really a living hell.

You were in it for the money?

Of course that was a big part, but at the time I was interested in the trade. I love the sensual world. Like an *oiran* from the Edo period.

Why did you give it up? What are you doing now?

Simply put, the agency wanted me to do more self-promotion and it soon became unpleasant for me because of that. I wasn't yet 20, so I quit on the basis that "adults are really scary."

At the moment I am employed in guarding my dwelling.

What did your parents think?

Oh, there's no way they'd know. Maybe they suspected it, but they have never said anything.

So you're a *hikikomori* NEET. But what about other jobs back then – wouldn't the wages seem pathetically low?

When I was doing the AVs I was also working part time at a shop at night, so I don't think it matters.

People's sense of money varies from person to person. If it was a job with easy interpersonal relations even 600 an hour would be fine, I think. But that's just what I think.

You don't seem to regret working in the world of AV. So as a security guard for your own residence are you still surviving on what you made then?

I do regret it. At one point I regretted it so much I became a wreck. But no matter how much you regret something it doesn't change the present. Maybe now I feel half regret, half a sense that it was the right thing to so. Maybe that's just me rationalizing it, or maybe I do feel that way, I don't know.

Was there a film you made which you have particular confidence in?

There is one I have real confidence in. Even I was like "Who is this, she's so *kawaiiii*!" The makeup and lighting were fantastic.

Did you tell your friends you were doing it? The guy with the DVDs, did he notice from watching them?

I was on all these magazines so I guess they saw it there. I was a slut from the start so people probably weren't exactly shocked, it was more like "if it's her it's no surprise she's doing it."

Why are you working as a home security guard? Aren't there things you'd like to do?

The reason I'm guarding is because human relationships are a real problem for me. Now I study a bit in my masses of spare time, even though I never studied at university.

There's not really anything I'd like to do. I'm more hoping for the world to end quickly.

Sorry about this one – you know the electro-massager AV stuff around? Is that really pleasurable? Isn't it too intense and just painful?

No, it's fine, I like this kind of gross dirty stuff. It depends on the person. Some hate them, some love them.

I'm the latter group. I bought one and it's pretty amazing, I come in 0.5 seconds just touching it to myself.

Did you ever eat excrement or have sex with animals?

I have never done either. I tried hard to become a hentai of that level but in the end it was no good.

I feel guilty receiving fellatio if I don't return the favor with cunnilingus.

I think any girl would be happy about that. It's proof you're thinking of the woman, isn't it? If you don't like it you'd better try hard to please with your cock.

Do big penises feel better? Are they all the same after a certain size and hardness? I'm losing pretty badly to those actors in this respect.

Big sizes do feel better than mini-sizes, for sure.

But this varies from person to person. Some even like them long and narrow, others short and stout.

Also there is the matter of physical compatibility, where

the size just doesn't matter – like a key fitting in a keyhole.

And more important than that is hardness. Hardness really matters.

Can you tell if an actress is faking it in a porn movie? Any tricks which help?

If they're going at it saying "an-an" all the time you can bet they are acting only. Nasal heavy breathing is another sign. Anything nasal really.

Frankly put, eighty percent of it is purely fake.

How old are you now?

I'm eternally 17 – it's too embarrassing to say otherwise.

When was your first time?

I was 13, in the winter. The guy was 9 years older. Now that I think of it, he was a *lolicon* wasn't he?

How did you end up with him?

We were drinking with friends and he hit on me, and we got to know each other much better. I was a slut from the start.

Japanese Brothel Manager #1

The following is a translation of another 2Chan interview with a manager of a brothel in Japan. The subject made himself available to answer the questions of the anonymous masses.

Delivery Health is a sort of outcall escort service that is very popular in the land of the rising sun. The subject of this interview managers such a shop.

I'm a man. Can you give me a job?

You can work as a driver, on the phones, or as a shop manager.

How are your profits?

Well, that depends on the trade. Good months can see us with 10,000,000 [around $100,000 US] left over.

You with a gang or the _yakuza_?

I was an amateur to start with. I just liked calling delivery girls over.

Are you feeling the effects of the recession?

Absolutely. We're OK but the trade as a whole has been hit hard.

What are your stats?

Graduated from middle school only. 34. I wasn't a delinquent or anything. This work is the most dodgy thing I've done. I'm average.

Tell us your career history and how you got your initial capital.

Middle school > Painter >Deliveryman > Plumber > Delivery Health Owner. The financing was of course from a consumer loan.

How much capital do you need?

At first about 2,000,000. With two shops, 5,000,000. If you wanted to completely avoid any chance of failure 10,000,000 would be best. It varies with the region I think.

Tell us the top 3 motivations of the girls.

Money. Money. Money.

Well, just why they need the money varies. There are surprisingly few who are in debt. Usually they just don't have any work. We often interview students.

So it's mostly girls after money to play around with?

For young girls who leave high school they can't even get dispatch work. They have no options except for the sex trade.

What do you do with troublesome customers? What have you done to them?

All we do for no good customers is not to deal with them again.

What are your advertising and operating costs?

A site is about ¥15,000-100,000, we use about 10. Sometimes magazines. All in all about 2,000,000 a month.

It seems many shops are moving over to delivery health only.

This varies with the region, but most new outfits are delivery health. Getting permission for shops is an issue. You just need to report your operation with a delivery health service, so there's still not much pressure.

Do you give the new girls erotic training?

For those we think it necessary for we do.

What about STDs? Do you do checks? If so how often?

Monthly. Nowadays you can do them through the mail. Send some urine and blood and you get the results back.

How much does the most popular princess work? How much does she earn?

The most popular works 20 days a month and takes home about 1,000,000-1,500,000 [around $12,850 US].

How much do you make?

I take home about 5,000,000 [around $51,500 US] monthly I think. I don't have that much use for it though so I only use 500,000 of that.

Tell us your work hours and holidays. Depending on your answer I may change my profession.

Usually 9AM-7PM. The late shift is 7PM to 5AM.

There is sometimes overtime. One day off a week. Wages are 250,000 to 1,500,000 depending on ability.

Where can I find this kind of work?

Magazines, job ads, homepages, that secret place. Try phoning them straight up and you may get an interview. I don't really recommend this kind of work though.

We put some ads up, got a lot of interest but mostly they failed to show for the interview, some were late, etc…

Blonde hair and brown hair are out. Thugs are out. People who can't use *keigo* are out. Uglies are out. People who can't greet properly are out. People with poorly written CVs are out. People late to interviews are out. Not really many you can employ.

I heard speeding customers or *yakuza* members are bad news. Do you get those types?

Been doing this 5 years, never had a customer like that. If there was we'd call the cops.

You sample the goods in the interviews?

No way.

Why not? Seems natural.

In the interview you're supposed to put them at ease and get them working for you. If you start with a fellataview or whatever they'd run out on you. If you're doing training you tempt the girls to come to you for it.

Training?

More things like time management than sexual technique.

Do you get a lot of cute young girls at the interviews?

Everything from minors to 50-year-old women. Mostly 20-35.

Do you have to pay the *yakuza*?

Not really. We have no contact with them.

Can customers go all the way with the women?

No. They're fired if they're caught. Of course they're alone with a guy at a hotel. Who knows what they do.

Are you paying taxes on that income of yours?

We get some trouble from the taxman, but there's all kinds of know how involved so it's quite safe.

What do you tell your folks?

That I'm self-employed, a little bit of real estate, some eateries... Mom and dad, I'm sorry.

I think when I graduate from uni I'll hire a girl and lose my virginity. Do you get annoying customers like that?

There are ones who tell us they're virgins. After hearing that I can't send them a funny girl.

You don't let homely girls work for you?

The world's not full of beautiful girls you know. There are some plain ones who get a lot of repeat customers. The really bad ones we drop at the interview though.

I had a girl in Osaka for 40 minutes and she spent 30 minutes chatting and 5 fellating. Get on with it!

We do get those kind of complaints – those kind of girls are fired. But not many customers complain to us like that.

Japanese are like that. Put up with the thing and bitch about it online.

Right. Hearing bad things about ourselves on 2chan and then having someone investigate our own girls secretly has happened.

What's your shop's theme?

We have 10 shops so there are all sorts, from normal to maniac.

Do you employ a scary body guards? Tell us about your weirder episodes with customers.

We do employ a scary bodyguard, but don't use him much. Strange customers… There was one who asked to be made to eat excrement, another had already soiled his diaper. We always get interesting ones dressed as ladies.

You have special relationships with cops? Do you pay them any "special fees"?

Not me, no. Just occasional encounters around… "You're not messing around are you now?" I never even considered any special fees. Doing that sort of thing in Japan is more dangerous than not.

Do you get stalkers?

If you leave them alone they get bored and go off somewhere, usually. The bad ones you can get angry at and threaten a bit. For real bad ones you can get the police in.

How much does delivery health cost?

The market rate is about 10-20,000 [around $155 US] for an hour, depending on the play content. Hotels cost extra. Expensive isn't it? At these prices I couldn't swindle our customers.

I get the impression the girl quality hierarchy goes from Cabaret Club > Soapland > Delivery Health > Pink Salon?

The soft service shops naturally get the prettiest girls, though maybe that is just because of the relative numbers looking to get in to each. Everyone tries to get into the cabaret club, but they only take the prettiest, so the rest have to interview down at a delivery health shop.

Japanese Brothel Manager #2

Delivery Health, or "delihel," is very popular in Japan. It is so popular that multiple delivery health managers have done question and answer sessions with the public.

This interview also appeared on 2Chan originally. It has been translated into English below to give readers a good sense of what things are like behind the scenes.

You only run delivery health?

Only delihel. Without going into details, when you see places where there are only delivery health it's usually because the area prohibits brothels by ordinance.

Tell us your income and stuff.

About 10,000,000 annually. Nothing special, I run it by myself. I can handle it by myself, but dealing with the girls and customer phone calls is nothing but hassle.

Are the outfits which run "VIP courses," like 25,000 for 90 minutes, offering girls who'll go all the way? Do those shops not report themselves to police?

I can't speak for all, but even among outfits that report to police many close their eyes to what girls do. The places which send you leaflets are reporting, no mistake. Our girls don't do it at all though.

So they're ignoring it. I tried a place with a VIP course which let you have sex with them as much as you like in the time limit, so I though they might all do it that way. Maybe it was just the girl.

Yeah. Girls might do it for money or fun. I don't know about shops which make girls do that.

But it's their responsibility, and if they do that the shop's image will be harmed so we strictly forbid it. Hardly any girls like that though.

I have a friend do a spy check on them to see what they get up to.

How much do you pay to the authorities?

Honestly, I pay some to the cops.

As a bodyguard type, do you have to be buff?

Sometimes I see girls to and from clients. I'm 170cm and quite slim. As long as you're not really frail it's fine. That sort of thing only happened to me once before.

You know any *yakuza*?

I know them.

When you start a shop up, do you have to speak to the yakuza organization?

I think you're OK with just the cops. If you're in with the *yakuza* it'll be nothing but trouble all the time. I tell them to be discreet.

Tell me your region and prices, and the names of your best 3 girls.

Saga prefecture. Fees are 15,000 for an hour. Telling you their names would give away who we are so I'll leave it at that.

How many girls do you have?

15 girls at the one shop. Usually 3-4 are at work. Later I expect it'll go up to 20.

Do you have new girls fellate you at interviews?

I've never done that. Our girls are mostly experienced in the sex trade.

How long do you work?

From the evening until 3-4AM, when the girls finish up.

I ran a delivery health shop before and when I told the girls my number a lot asked me for loans. Are there a lot of them who have financial problems?

Our girls are young and want to live luxuriously, and a lot of the girls want to get rich quick. Most of them are from normal homes rather than poor ones.

What are the employment criteria for your girls? Looks? Manners?

Honestly, I don't check manners and just prioritize looks. Ugly fatties are definitely out. They're a nuisance to cute girls too.

What is the split? Half and half?

Yes, roughly half and half.

How much do you spend on magazine and prostitution site advertising? A lot of them give discounts if you say you saw the ad there, do they work well?

I spend about 400,000 on advertising. About 10,000-30,000 per site. If you aren't on popular sites, customers won't come. At first I didn't know what was effective, so I spent more on things like magazine ads.

How many johns do you get each day and when do they come?

For us it's 100% night customers. If it goes well, it maxes out about 21, but it can be as low as 5.

How many johns on average?

9-10.

As boss what exactly do you do ordinarily?

Handling phone calls, checking on the girls' work, updating the site, meeting them or sending them off. We only have 3 people so I end all doing a bit of everything.

Do you do a lot to provide a good working environment? Do anything for their mental well-being? I get the impression some girls are pretty flaky. What about you?

You don't really know how they will do until they start. There was one girl with mental problems. She was cutting her wrists, so I had her quit after a week. Maybe there's a better way, but I only take any notice of the stuff on the outside.

What happens to the girls who quit? How do they move on?

I don't ask what happens to them when they quit. Most of the girls doing this are sluts so I doubt they can get out of the business.

Have you been burned by any customers?

Some want forbidden acts or excessively perverted stuff.

What are the most difficult things about your job?

There's no future in sight, and I can never tell my parents what I do.

I make tons of cash though so I have no intention of quitting.

Do you take precautions against STDs?

Honestly, I think they're an unavoidable part of the business. Generally we have the girls go to the hospital for a checkup once a month.

What gets girls wanting to do this work?

In this day and age, there's no particular reason or set of circumstances.

As I was saying, the girls mostly want to get rich quick and can't hold a regular job. Many say they want their own shop, but basically the reasons are as stated above.

Do things ever get hairy?

I once took a punch – I had to stop a customer who was demanding full sex from a girl.

You have any girls no guys would be pleased to see?

We drop really bad ones at interview, but yes, there are some girls who are neither good nor bad.

Is there really that much demand for this? With hotel fees and extra charges for sex it comes to 20,000 a time.

Near my house there's a place with rooms which gives full sex and 40 minutes for only 10,000. Shouldn't you be adding value with fetish play, BDSM, and so on?

I keep saying it, but we don't let girls have sex with customers.

As to the shop, I don't know any like that. We make a lot from having girls who behave amateurishly and give a sham romance type experience.

Do you use your own shop?

Use my own shop? Never.

Cam Model Cammi Cams

While she obviously does not have the most creative name ever conjured up, Cammi Cams is one of the better known adult webcam models around. Starting out as an amateur she now runs a website and has all sorts of followers. She also sells her own porn videos which means she has graduated to porn starlet level too. The following is an interview I did with her back in 2015.

How old are you and where are you from?

I say forever 35 but my birthday is March 20 and I was born in California.

When did you first have sex? When did you first see porn?

I was 16.

When did you first become aware of adult webcams?

Ever since I started dancing in gentlemen's clubs.

How and when did you start doing them?

I starting being a webcam model full time back in June 1 2007.

You seem to be very popular and it's easy to figure out why. Did you you think you would do as well as you have when you first got into adult entertainment?

Yes! Because I have been in the adult industry for many years and know how to entertain men.

Can porn still make money in the era of tube sites? A lot of women in porn are now doing things like webcam shows and feature dancing. On the other hand I see a lot of cam models like you and Anna Bell Peaks doing videos so there must still be something to it.

Being live will always win over videos in my opinion. I make the best videos possible with what I have. So that my fans have something to watch when I am not on cam.

You offer custom videos on your site. This is very interesting and seems to me to be a way to make good income. Is this a popular option for your fans?

No not really I get one or two a month.

How long does it take you to put a video together and what does it cost?

It could take up to two days and it cost $50 for 5 minutes and $100 for a 10 to 15 minute video.

Your boobs are pretty big. What size are they?

34DD.

Have you always been busty?

Nope I was a 34A.

Are you ever recognized on the street?

Yes, two times.

Have you or would you ever date a fan?

No! I would just do a meet-n-greet at an adult show when and if I can ever afford it.

Do your friends and family know about your work?

Yes.

Do you have a boyfriend?

Yes thousands of my cyber-sex fans.

What advice would you have for someone who wanted to get into camming or selling porn videos online?

Have a goal, a business plan and a thick skin. Don't make this a career and don't be afraid to use your ban button for those haters.

What's the best thing about doing adult cam shows?

The money.

What's the worst?

The freeloaders and haters

What's your favorite adult webcam site?

Mine!

How often do you broadcast?

Six days a week seven hours a day and two to three hours on Saturday.

Does the income you make from camming surpass what you would make from a "regular" day job? Do you think the majority of cam models make as much as you do?

Yes unfortunately it has to or I lose everything.

How long do you plan on entertaining your fans?

Until the day I have my bills paid off or have a normal job which pays the same!

Do you have any ideas about doing other things in the future?

I would love to own an adult site or have a normal job that makes enough money so I can stop being on cam.

Thanks a lot for answering these questions. Where can readers see more of you?

I am live on my site CammiCams.com.

Porn Producer Mr Nuttz

Mr Nuttz is the stage name of a self-made porn producer who markets his work on sites like Clips4Sale. He is an interesting and prolific guy who was more than willing to open up for the following interview.

How old are you and where are you from?

I am in my late 40's & I am originally from the great state of Louisiana but I reside in Detroit, Michigan.

How did you get into shooting porn? How long have you been doing it?

An ex girlfriend that I met in the lifestyle got the filming all started. I have been doing amateur porn for 8 years now.

Is the porn industry difficult to navigate? What are some of the obstacles to shooting your own porn?

It's not difficult for me at all. I do things my way, always have. A lot of people get caught up in equipment, co-stars, & things of that nature. Hardcore quality sex is what the buyers are looking for. Give them that and they will be happy.

Where do you find models? Have you ever had issues with models wanting their videos taken down after you post them online? Have you ever run into models that were unable to perform due to things like diseases or poor hygiene?

Honestly, I don't have to find models anymore, most of them find me. It's a nice change of pace. On the amateur circuit there are always going to be mishaps & change of hearts. Two of my most successful partners asked if I could remove their videos from my studio. And out of respect I had to oblige.

You sell your videos through Clips4Sale. I've mentioned Clips4Sale several times on this site over the years including once in a post on porn that's still worth paying for. I think you can find a lot of unique content there. How did you find the site and how does selling there work out for you?

I have been on clips4sale since it's early existence. A hardcore fan base dwells there & that's one of the reasons I do so well there. My studio has been exclusively at the number one spot since they have started the rankings a few years ago, and I wouldn't be there if I wasn't making good money.

Can you still make money with porn? How true are the rumors that free porn has killed the industry?

No matter how much they flood the market with booze, drugs and sex, it will always sell.

How long ago did you first see porn? How do you think it has changed since then?

I was introduced to porn at a early age by staying up late at night and watching cable TV. It has changed vastly, no such thing as a plot, wardrobe, or even acting.

Do your family and friends know that you shoot porn?

I told the ones that need to know. Besides that, no one else really knows. If they were told they probably wouldn't believe it.

Is it difficult to date if you produce porn?

Well making it and producing it is really two different things. I now own Mr Nuttz Productions and I edit and produce for multiple talents. The time I spend on others outweighs the time I spend on my own studio. But once you get a strong talent it can be very rewarding.

What advice would you have for anyone who wanted to follow your footsteps? If it was a friend or family member would the advice change at all?

If it was a friend or family member I would tell them to join the military. Besides that, I would tell everyone to own your own content. Working for a big porn company sounds exciting, but they will own the footage of you forever and you have no say so and get no residuals. Be your own boss. Independence is paramount!

Who was the best model you ever filmed? Which scene was the best?

Are the scenes you like the most the scenes that sell the best? Well, I enjoy filming with the females in my network, especially the ones that worked with me when I was up & coming. I am very loyal to those who have been with me from the beginning. The scenes that you think are going to be a flop usually are a hit, and the sure fire classics end up being duds. It's not what you like, it's what your supporters like!!!

How long do you plan on producing porn?

The light is at the end of the tunnel. I don't have too much time left and I prefer to leave with a respectful reputation and work ethic.

What was the last book you read? What's your favorite movie?

Debt Of Honor, Tom Clancy. Favorite movie? Wow, that's a tough one since I am a serious movie critic. Comedy: *Blazing Saddles*. Western: *The Good, The Bad & The Ugly*. Suspense: *Mystic River*. Action: *Matrix / Terminator* (original).

Where can readers find out more about you?

I love any kind of response from you guys. The patronage and support that I get from across the globe is overwhelming and sometimes very humbling. You can view me and contact me at any of the given. I thank you for the opportunity to grace your site and I hope at least one person gets a better view of who I am and what I do.

Porn Star Anna Belle Peaks

Anna Bells Peaks is now a well known porn star in the United States. When I interviewed her she was up and coming. She started out as an adult webcam model but moved into porn. Clearly people saw something in Anna which led to her success. As far as I can tell that is continuing. She regularly does scenes and they all get a good response.

How old are you and where are you from?

I am 33 years old originally from the Midwest part of the country.

How did you get into adult entertainment? Did you start with adult webcams?

Yes, it started with just dabbling part time in web camming at night after working my old full time job. I enjoyed it so much (and made more money haha) that I decided to cam full time. The adult films started almost immediately after I decided to cam full time. That was November 2014.

What do you think your best physical feature is? Besides your looks what do you think makes you popular?

People tell me its my tits or my smile. I think I am popular on cam because I am genuine, nice, and eager to please everyone who enters my room. I'm drama free, love sex, and generally was raised to be nice to everyone and respectful of men.

How big are your boobs? Are they real?

Size 32G, they are fake. Pre-surgery I had large breasts, so my fake tits look very real and are quite soft and fun to play with!

How many tattoos do you have? When did you get your first?

I have 27 tattoos, got my first one at 18, a tiny butterfly on my shoulder.

What is your private sex life like? Is it wild and crazy or vanilla?

I have always had an active and wild private sex life. I love to talk dirty and spice things up in the bedroom.

After spotting you on MyFreeCams I caught you in a video on Clips4Sale doing full sex in a superhero costume. Many of the most popular cam girls seem to do Clips4Sale videos nowadays. How did you get into that?

When I cam, its fairly easy to record the live shows I perform. I also make custom vids for individual men. Once these videos are made, I can easily upload them for sale on Clips4Sale for so many more men to enjoy and it provides an additional income stream for me. I try to make new videos every week or two so there is more content available.

I recently heard that you shot a scene for Reality Kings. Is that right? Do you have plans to expand to any other areas of entertainment? What should we look forward to?

I have now already shot with Reality Kings, Bang Bros, Naughty America, Evil Angel, and Burning Angel, and am headed out to Vegas and LA again March 23-31st for more shoots with additional companies. I hope to take the adult film industry by storm and bring a fresh face, bold look, and confident sexy woman to the screen.

Have you ever stripped?

No. Scratch that. I did it one day, for fun, just to see what it was like!

Does camming or doing videos for things like Clips4Sale pay better?

Camming pays better. For me. I'm told I'm quite lucky to be so successful, but I honestly attribute it to the fact that I am nice, I please men, and people can see that I really enjoy myself.

I was talking to a cam model who told me she makes 10 times what she made at her old full time office job now. Is this the norm or is she a special case? Do you think the work is much easier than a "regular job"? How long do you plan on doing it?

I make WAY more as a cam model then at my old job, and I had a great previous job in the business world. The work is not easier, its just different. At my old job I used my brain and didn't talk to tons of people. Now I talk to men every moment I'm online, and that takes skills; to be resilient if someone isn't so nice, to have fun and be willing to try new things, and to treat each person special.

What advice would you have for someone who wanted to follow in your footsteps? Would the advice change if a relative or friend of yours asked?

If you want to be a full time cam model, know that working

isn't an 8-5 M-F work schedule like in the business world. There are days I work til 4 or 5am, and days i log off at midnight because its slow. The key is consistency. I try to log 40 hours ON CAMERA every week! Then add to that hours spent on twitter and snapchat and instagram and updating spreadsheets with lists, editing videos I made, uploading content to websites. Its HARD WORK to be successful. But my goal is to be #1. Not #25, not just a big name on cam or in porn. NUMBER 1. And I'm driven and dedicating my hours to reach that goal.

Do your friends and family know about your work?

No, right now very few friends and no family know about my work, but I know that will change in the near future.

What do you think about prostitution?

I generally disagree with the notion. I would not wish to be "forced" to have sex with someone for money. Prostitution implies that the woman HAS TO have sex because they are being paid for it. I would rather choose my sexual partners. Hope that makes sense.

Why do you think camming is still so popular even though there is so much free porn available online and indeed even captures of live cam shows?

One on one interaction and the idea that something a man in my room says to me turns me on or makes me cum, or that by tipping, they were able to make my show start. Its the individual contact.

Have you ever or would you ever consider dating or fucking someone who you met while camming?

Maybe. I would consider a date raffle, in fact Ill be doing my first one April 25th in FL, so I hope it turns out OK.

What kind of panties are you wearing right now?

None. I seem to have sold all my panties online recently and in severe need of a trip to Victoria Secret!

What are your favorite books and movies?

Ayn Rand *Atlas Shrugged*, *The Fountainhead*. Also *Pride and Prejudice*, *Jane Eyre*. *Phantom of the Opera*.

Do you have anything else to say to my readers? Where can they see more of you?

Find me on Twitter @redandwild0

Porn Star Anna Belle Peaks

Miko Dai is an Asian-American porn starlet who quickly rose to prominence after putting out a number of scenes. I was intrigued the first time I saw her. I reached out to her for an interview and thankfully she agreed. The very interesting results follow.

When and how did you get into porn?

I did my first shoot early August of 2014. I really didn't intend to stay in the industry, as I was in law school at the time– Georgia State University (on summer break) and did not plan to leave. I saw on ad on the internet that advertised to fly girls down to Miami to do a few paid shoots (for a pretty substantial sum.. I think the ad said $5,000). I have been in the adult industry for about 5 years: I started dancing at a local gentlemen's club when I was 20, so it wasn't a huge leap for me to make a trip down to Florida, earn some quick cash, and return to school a week or two later.

When I got to Florida, I started shooting and things sort of just happened really fast. I had a few realizations 2 or so weeks into shooting that made me rethink going back to law school– and ultimately I made the decision to pursue a career in porn instead of returning to school.

A; I liked having sex in front of the camera and was comfortable working with talent, crew, director, etc.

B; porn is film making: There was an art to it that I hadn't quite realized or acknowledged until I was in front of the camera. I wanted to learn more.

C; everyday was an adventure.

D; quitting school and doing porn would be the biggest risk I've ever taken. At my age (25), this was my only opportunity to pursue this. So I did.

E; I was bored with life and scared to death that I would end up hating my life, job, and myself (years down the road). Porn allowed me to do things, meet people, have experiences that I would never have the chance to encounter otherwise.

What sets you apart from other people who do porn?

I think my academic background, age and ethnicity are my most defining/unique traits as an adult performer. I have a degree in Economics from Emory University and (as I mentioned earlier) I went to law school for a year. I definitely know of girls in the industry who have gone to college, are working on their degrees, and/or have graduate degrees, but we are definitely in the minority. That being said, diplomas and education are not by any means a sole indicator of intelligence. I have met many intelligent women who don't have a high school degree. I'm also 25– which is pretty old to just be entering the industry. I stay in model houses when I shoot in LA (I plan on moving out West once my lease is up next month), so I meet a lot of girls in the industry. Most of them are in the 18-22 age group and I'm usually one of the oldest girls.

I notice that you publicly describe yourself as an humanist and say that having sex on camera is empowering. Can you give me a better idea of what you mean by this?

Humanism: One of the main tenants of humanism focuses on the inherent value of human beings and our ability, as social creatures, to empathize, communicate and take care of one another. These are ideals that I personally align with, as they are grounded in reason, logic and pragmatism, rather than "faith". That being said, I have no issue with mysticism, religion, or any kind of faith-based ideologies. The point of contention (for me) lies in that (most) organized religions create barriers and (unfairly) antagonize and marginalize certain groups of people. A very general example would be the controversy surrounding gay marriage. Why is this even an issue? The conservative argument is based solely on Judeo-Christian principals that (in my personal opinion) have no place in a "secular" nation (see Treaty of Tripoli).

Sexual Empowerment: Sex is empowering for me because I have used it to financially support myself, explore taboo subjects (that I find intriguing), and learn about the sex industry and how it works. In a way, being in this industry has made me more honest with myself and others.

Has porn changed since you first go into the industry?

I have only been in the industry for about 4 months so not a lot has changed. I do know, however, (pre-2007) before tube & stream sites emerged, porn was a much more fast paced, glamorous, and lucrative industry.

If you could start over again would you still have made porn?

Yes. 100%.

When did you watch your first porn? Do you remember it?

I first watched porn when I was 14. I had just had my first kiss the summer before 9th grade and I wanted to learn how to give a blow job– err, probably because I had told all my friends already that I had given a blow job and it was necessary to do the proper research to keep up the lie.

Anyway, I went on Limewire and downloaded a Naughty America scene with a beautiful, Aryan looking couple: the busty blonde woman with pigtails was the student and her co-talent was her teacher, a muscly, spiky haired blonde man with a soul patch. The main thing I remember is forgetting all about the blow job when I started watching, because the guy started eating the woman out, and I was like — mind blown. And that led to me getting slightly obsessed with cunnilingus and I started watching lesbian porn, which led to gay porn, which led to gang bangs....

What's your best sexual memory? What's your worst?

My best sexual memory happened recently when I was fooling around with a friend and he let me stick my finger up his butt! Prostate play has always intrigued me, but my sex life up until a couple months ago was SUPER vanilla. I never got to be adventurous with a partner that was comfortable enough with his sexuality to do things like that.. until porn.

My worst sexual memory is when I was 15 and I had snuck out of my house to meet this boy, who lived in my neighborhood, at the lake (our subdivision had a big fake lake in the middle of it). We sat by the water and made out for a little bit. And then we started getting more into it and I was like.. *ohhh I would look so sexy if I straddled him right now.. now is as good a time as ever to try dry humping!* So I straddled him, grinded on him and let him feel me up. His 5 inch cock was rock hard and I was soaking wet. I felt like the sexiest teenager in the world until I got up after and realized I was I bled all over his cargo pants (the ones with the huge pockets from Hollister). Epic fail.

When did you give your first blowjob? How was it?

I gave my first blowjob at the end of year party, my sophomore year of high school. It was the first night I had ever gotten

129

"wasted". My classmate's older brother who was a freshman in college came and I blew him in the coat closet. I don't remember too much, but I know, 1) he never came and 2) he never ate me out after like he promised.

If you had all the money you could ever want or need, would you still have done porn?

I probably would have tried it. I don't know if I would have stayed.

Have you had any issues with family or friends finding out about your porn work? Has it caused any problems in your personal life?

My ex-boyfriend recently (like 2 days after X-mas), emailed my parents and outed my porn career to them. It was a particularly spineless thing to do, especially since we stayed together almost 4 months after I started. My career wasn't even a huge contributing factor (except for the distance) to our break up: we were just two different people. And also I got tired of faking my orgasms with him.

Anyway, the day that he told my parents, we had talked on the phone earlier, argued and I ended up blocking his number. I guess he got desperate and emailed my parents.. because he's a snitch.

My parents found out, confronted me, and we're not really speaking at the moment. I wrote a blog entry in the form of a letter to them on my tumblr.

What advice would you give someone who wanted to get into porn? Would the advice be any different to a stranger than it would be to a sister or close friend?

It would be the same to anyone that wants to enter the business–

whether family or stranger– If you feel degraded, then don't do it. If it empowers you, inspires you, makes you feel good, then go for it.

What do you think about prostitution? You say you are a marijuana enthusiast. I was surprised that it was actually legalized in some parts of the US. I never thought I would see that in my lifetime. Do you think that prostitution will ever be legalized?

Prostitution in some form or another exists. I believe it should be legalized. I can only hope that our society becomes open minded enough to accept it.

Have you ever tried stripping or adult webcamming? How was it?

See answer to 1st question for dancing. I have done webcamming and in fact, I have a MyFreeCams account (mikodaixxx). I enjoy doing it, but I haven't had time to log in any real hours recently (because of holidays, work, life, etc).

Are you ever recognized in the street?

One time a person asked if I was that girl from the internet.

Do you think the average porn star makes more or less money over their career than they would have if they done a "regular" job instead?

I think an average porn star definitely makes more money than what an "average" job would bring in; however, the expense of being a porn star — basic maintenance/upkeep like nails, make up, working out, buying new outfits for shoots and travel — is considerably more expensive than just working a 9-5. These expenses can be partially reimbursed through taxes, however. It all kind of evens out in the end and I don't think one kind of worker is necessarily in a significant better financial situation than the other.

What kind of panties are you wearing right now?

No panties, hello kitty robe.

Do you ever have sex with random guys?

Not really. I used to be all about waking up next to an unfamiliar face in college. Now I'm okay with just focusing on work and having fun with my friends/colleagues, if the opportunity presents itself....

Does being in porn change the way you use social media? Can you still use things like Facebook to share pictures and chat with friends and family members without having it tied in to your porn?

Porn definitely introduced me to Twitter. I never had a twitter or even liked the idea of it before I started porn. Now, tweeting and staying on top of my social media (as Miko Dai) is an integral part of my job and building my career. When I started porn, I deleted all my "Kat" (that's my real name) social media accounts. I just recently started a Facebook with my real name, since my parents already know and I'd like to be able to keep in touch with old friends and classmates.

Porn Producer Mark Rockwell

In my view, Clips4Sale is one of real bright spots in an otherwise dwindling porn industry. The site allows producers to market their own scenes at their own prices. A lot of the content that comes out is low quality or even boring but there are also some real high points. No matter what one thinks, it would be difficult to deny the high production value and quality of the scenes put out by "Mark's Head Bobbers and Hand Jobbers."

This Clips4Sale studio has been releasing scene after scene for years. I reached out to the guy behind it to get some more information. Here are the results.

When did you see your first porn? What was it?

I was around 8 or 9 and was visiting my grandparents in Baltimore. My grandparents owned a few video stores and they had small adult sections in each, so they had quite a bit of adult videos in their TV room inside of their house. Obviously I wasn't supposed to know where they hid the smut, nor was I suppose to be watching them, but my brother and I found them and would always sneak in their TV room at night time and watch porn. I don't remember what video I saw first but I do remember it starred Tori Welles… I was hooked!

How long have you been shooting porn? How did you get into it?

I've been shooting for about three years now. Honestly, I have no idea how I started. I slowly started to research video equipment and before I knew it I was purchasing it.

Why did you choose to sell clips rather than going the more traditional route of setting up a membership website?

Clips4sale is a great platform to sell content, it's easy to set up, and they do a lot of the leg work for you, plus the site has a significant amount of daily traffic… so there is an opportunity to be very successful. I still think I may set up my own site in the future, but for now I'm pretty comfortable with where I am.

Your videos are of really good quality. Is that because you use good equipment or because you are simply a great videographer?

I've went through three to four different cameras and 5 different light sets to finally get to where I am now, and I'll probably change it up again. I appreciate the kind words, but I don't consider myself a great videographer, I'm learning as I go. However, I am a bit of a perfectionist so I am always trying to get better and the slightest flaws in my videos really piss me off… so I'm constantly trying to improve.

Did you learn how to shoot video by doing porn or is it a skill you already had that you brought to porn?

I definitely learned as I was shooting. Shooting POV is actually quite difficult… so it took a lot of trial and error. I try my best to get a nice steady shot and a mixture of angles that I think the viewer would enjoy.

Are you the only actor in the videos? Or do you bring in other guys from time to time?

If it's a POV clip, it is always me. I have used a black male talent twice and I used another talent for a double BJ one time… other than that it's all me!

Do you worry about STDs? Have you ever been burned by one of the models in your videos?

As long as you stick with the industries protocol and are smart about what you do off camera the risk should be very low.

What is the best scene you've done in your opinion?

That's a tough one. "Ultimate edge play" with Sasha Foxxx is my all time best seller. In fact, I have four scenes with Sasha and they have all done extremely well, people just really like her. Plus, she is incredibly good at POV clips and teasing... she understands how to be sensual and how to use her face during POV scenes. If you haven't checked her out I highly suggest you do! Her twitter is @foxxxstudios and she has her own clips4sale studio. Also, my ruined orgasm clips with Sarah Diavola have been extremely popular, especially "Sarah leaves you in ruins". Sarah is an amazing performer and really knows how to play to the camera. Everything I shoot with her turns to gold! Her twitter is @sarahdiavola and she has her own clips4sale studio. Lastly, my ruined orgasm scene with Jade Indica, "Jade leaves you in ruins". Jade has a very exotic look and is a very talented performer, she knows what's hot and how to use her body and face during POV scenes.

What's the most popular material in your store?

Definitely my edging blowjob and hand job scenes as well as my ruined orgasm scenes. Those are by far my best selling genres.

What have you changed since you started?

I started off focusing on doing blow jobs with big facials, I though that would be my best selling point with my massive pop. But after doing a few teasing/edging clips I found that they sold 20 times better, I would have never guessed that! I should note that the clips on Kilxen's studio inspired me to start the slower edging scenes. She and her male partner, who I am guessing is her husband, are both incredible at what they do. I have done my best not to steal their style but make it my own by the way I shoot the content, the positioning of the girls, and incorporating feet, pantyhose, and other leg wear.

Can porn still make enough money to support itself? What is the future of the industry and what role do the tube sites play?

Tube sites are a poison to the industry as well are torrent sites.....PERIOD.

What advice do you have for people who want to make their own porn? What if they want to make a living at it?

You have to find your niche. Having a talent to bring to the table isn't a bad idea either... big cum shot, huge cock, awesome video and editing skills, etc. If you are good at what you do and are able to market it, you can be VERY successful.

What kind of advice do you have for guys that want to shoot ropes like we see in your videos?

I think my cum shot is purely genetic. I try not to ejaculate for at least three days before I shoot, to ensure I have a good first pop. Other than that I don't have any real secrets. Some male performers take zinc pills to help out but I didn't really notice any difference in my cum shots while I was taking it.

Do you have anything to say to the readers of this site? Where can they find out more about you?

I really appreciate all of my customers that buy my content. I also love getting e-mails, it doesn't matter if it's a compliment, request, or even to let me know that you didn't like a clip of mine... all feedback helps me to improve my craft. My e-mail is trueamature@gmail.com and my twitter is @bjsandhjs. Lastly, I would say if you are finding yourself getting bored with mainstream porn... give Clips4sale and other amateur sites a try. It's a nice change of pace and if you're into specific niches/fetishes you'll be more likely to find it in the amateur arena.

Internet Porn Star MyCherryCrush

The internet has changed nearly every aspect of life. From its earliest days it changed porn. Besides making the stuff so easily available it also gave rise to independent producers and performers. MyCherryCrush is one such person who made a living by selling her own videos after first rising to prominence in the adult webcam scene.

How old are you and where are you from?

I'm 24, I am from Miami originally but I move around a lot.

Could you tell us how and when you got into porn?

I used to be a cam girl about 2 years go and got really into it. Then I got a high demand for making videos. So eventually had a lot of content and decided to open my website.

It seems like you went your own way in porn. Do you shoot all of your own material and only shoot with one guy, or am I off base?

Yea everything is my own material, I shoot with my boyfriend and sometimes other cam girls

Have you ever tried stripping?

No I haven't, I think it would not be my thing.

Did you ever consider going out to "porn valley" or Miami and working with one of the big studios?

Not really, no. I've gotten offers but I'm rather settled with the path I've taken.

Speaking of that, do you think porn can continue to be profitable with all of the free content now available online? What is the future of the industry?

I think sex will always sell. Even though there are many tube sites out there, a lot of people still like high quality content and don't mind contributing to keep them going. I don't know what the future of the industry will be but hopefully it involves some virtual reality stuff.

If you could start over again would you still have made porn?

Yes indeed I love where my life has taken me. Doing porn has made my life better in other areas as well. I am much healthier than when I started, I quit smoking, I eat better and exercise regularly. I feel much more centered now.

Have you had any issues with family or friends finding out about your porn work? Has it caused any problems in your personal life?

In the beginning it was weird with my parents, they didn't like it. Slowly they started to understand what I am doing and that I am able to support myself through it. I am not hurting myself or anyone and I am not doing anything illegal. They are just careful not to run into any pics or vids online.

When did you watch your first porn? Do you remember it?

The first porn I watched was when I was 13, my friend's brother was watching it and I walked in on him.

I believe it was a 3-way school girl porn with an older couple, haha.

What's the best sexual position?

Reverse cowgirl or doggy style

You give an excellent blowjob, or at least know how to make it look excellent on camera. How did you develop that skill? Do you remember your first blow job?

I think I just naturally have an oral fixation, I have fun with it and enjoy it. I do remember, it was really awkward and I made him wear a condom. I was really bad at it and very prude haha.

What do you think of extreme porn? Gang bangs, bondage, bukkake, gokkun, etc. How about Japanese porn?

Group sex isn't my thing, when I watch porn I tend to watch more role-playing stuff.

What do you think about prostitution?

I feel that sex workers can give someone attention, a feeling of being wanted. Even if it's just an act, they are still making that person feel happy. I wouldn't do it myself mostly because I wouldn't feel comfortable but if someone wanted to then it's their choice. Nothing wrong with that.

Are you ever recognized when you're out?

I am very good at being incognito.

I've been spotted a few times though.

What are your favorite websites and apps?

YouTube, Netflix mostly and probably every social media app.

Thanks for doing this interview. Where can readers find out more about you?

Thank you.

My website is mycherrycrush.com, You can also follow me on twitter @mycherrycrush.

Porn Star Nautica Thorn

Nautica Thorn is a very interesting person. She rose through the ranks of the American porn industry in the earlier days of widespread internet use. She became very well known when porn stars were still really stars. Yet she continued in the new atmosphere that arose around her. I was more than happy to interview her and I can't think of a more fitting person to close this volume with.

I'm sure you've been asked this countless times but could you tell us how and when you got into porn?

I got into porn when I was 18 going on 19. I was a dancer on the famous Sunset Strip in Los Angeles. It's funny how it worked out. First one of my regular customers was a warehouse worker for Vivid Entertainment and then an agent came up to me about some modeling. Everything was pretty much history after that.

Are you still making porn now?

I work for myself. I am currently updating my website EnterNautica.com and doing a show a week on cammodels.com

How has porn changed since you first go into the industry?

I feel it has changed in a sense that the generation I was in was one of the last that did it as a job that we enjoyed. Now I think it veered into a direction of just a money opportunity. Yes the money is great and potential for a girl to really market herself if she surrounded herself with good people, but we also loved what we did. That's what makes great porn. You could be hot as fuck but if your just laying there, I'll find someone else to watch.

If you could start over again would you still have made porn?

Yes. I was and am still a very open minded and adventurous person. So I know I would have made the same choice. And I don't think I would be the person I am today and my life experiences without it. So no regrets and no do overs. I would do the same thing.

When did you watch your first porn? Do you remember it?

I think I was 15 or so. It was Asia Carrea.

What's your best sexual memory? What's your worst?

This question is easy, haha. My best was in Hawaii, on Tantalus, and having a sex marathon. The guy I was with wanted to see how many times he could make me cum. I lost count after 10. That night was by far my favorite. As for my worst......There are surprisingly too many to name.

When did you give your first blowjob? How was it?

First off I have a very high oral fixation, so with that said I'm pretty sure I gave my first blow job when I first had sex. I don't remember but I know me and she would do that.

If you had all the money you could ever want or need, would you still have done porn?

Yes. I wouldn't have changed anything.

Have you had any issues with family or friends finding out about your porn work? Has it caused any problems in your personal life?

No. I have been fortunate to have very good friends. I surround myself with only positive people. As for family, of course there was the shock and disappointment, but in the end I was born and raised in Hawaii. We are a very family tight culture. So everything was back to normal when the dust settled.

What would your advice be to a person wanting to get into porn now? If it was a sister or family member asking, would your advice change?

My advice I gave all girls that asked for my opinion was first and foremost, now that you had a thought about getting into this industry, think about how it'll impact you. Think about what you'll tell your family and friends (cause they will find out), think about employment after, think about what your tell your future family of your own. All these questions girls don't think about before making a decision. Hell no one told me. It wouldn't have changed my mind of doing it, but it would have made me approach the industry different and I would have set myself up different and had a better exit plan.

The Guy Behind the Filipina Candy Porn Website

Filipina Candy is one of many pornographic websites on the internet that focuses on Filipina women. Although there are now many websites of this type, Filipina Candy was definitely one of the first. The guy behind the website developed a reputation over the years. I was very pleased to interview him to get his outlook on the website and other aspects of life.

What made you get into porn?

It was a natural progression starting way back when I first bought a swingers magazine filled with personal ads looking to trade pictures through the mail. I started trading pictures and that grew to trading VHS tapes (Yes VHS, which was a long time ago). Years later the computer revolution came and I saw some of the same people I was trading photos/videos with on the internet and I began contributing to their sites. I was suddenly being asked to become a content provider because I had Asian porn that at the time was very rare.

How long has your site been online? How often is it updated?

Filipina Candy has only been online for less than two years; however I have been a content producer for magazines and websites since 1993. After being a content provider for many years and having accumulated a vast trove of images and videos I decided to start a small website. I have so many images that I can update weekly for years to come, but I still film all the time.

Do you shoot with Filipina models because they work for less than some others, because you find them more beautiful, because the content sells, or for some other reason?

I never got into the business for profit. It was all just fun for me. If you include the air travel, taxis, hotels, dining, dating and daily expenses it is cheaper to film in the USA. Actually, porn models in the USA are a dime a dozen in California. I don't just film Filipina girls. I am still a producer of Korean, Japanese, and Thai for other sites but I love hunting down amateur Filipinas to film for my own site.

How well does your site perform, financially speaking? What advice do you have for guys who want to start producing porn?

FilipinaCandy.com does well because it is a niche market having strictly pinay models, but you are never going to be really rich in the porn industry. However, there are sites that spend 10's-100's of thousands of dollars in marketing (with all their pop up ads, SEO consultants, buying every banner space they can, making hundreds of redundant websites and TGP/FHG, creating fake review sites, making fake forum boards, etc.) and they do very well.

As far as guys wanting to start producing porn I would say that there is always room for more entrepreneurs but most of the markets are pretty saturated because of tube sites stealing your content and giving it away for free, and as I said the marketing moguls who over advertise makes a start up producers job very difficult.

What do you think of Filipina porn stars in America like Lucky Starr, Annie Cruz and Lana Croft?

Lucky Starr is in her 40's. Wasn't she arrested for prostitution a

146

few years back? That says it all! None of them could even get hired as a whore in any bar in the Philippines because they are ugly. Who wants to see scripted moaning and set up conversations? I guess some people do. I like young amateurs who have sex for fun and have real orgasms.

When did you first travel to Asia? The Philippines?

I came to Asia in the 80's and have lived all over South and East Asian countries. I first came to the Philippines in the 90's and it is one of my favorite places, however the crime rate is so high I prefer developed nations like Korea, Okinawa or Hong Kong to live.

What do you think about prostitution?

I don't really engage that much with prostitutes anymore because there are girls everywhere and all it takes is learning the language and being outgoing. You would be surprised to know that Asian girls like foreigners just as much as we find them exotic. It doesn't hurt that they know you have a bigger dick and more money than a short, dark skinned, poor ass local.

Having said all that, I find it to be a victimless crime and the crime that is symbiotically associated with it is about the same as any other occupation. You probably get ripped off more by your local mechanic who cheats you on parts and labor than a prostitute in Asia. Bars in Asia control their workers very well and have weekly VD checks, unlike USA hookers who are drug addicts and carry diseases.

Prostitution in Asia has been around since time began and it does not have the same stigma that US Christian cock blockers try to portray that all sex workers are slaves and forced into prostitution. That is a complete fable.

The UN says prostitution should be legalized in the Philippines. What do you think about that?

The UN is fully aware that it cannot be eradicated because it is protected by politicians, police and the simple fact that the Philippines is a third world country with very high unemployment, terrible education systems where a great many never finish high school and have few opportunities. It is worth noting that unemployment is so bad that they have 2.2 million OFW (Overseas Foreign Workers). In other words, people have to travel to other countries to find work. Now top that with Philippine monthly salaries being just a few hundred dollars. When you are extremely poor and uneducated prostitution is just a job and it pays very well for very little work. The UN is aware that there is no such thing as forced sex labor camps as liberal bible thumpers like to preach. A girl from the province can make more money in one day than her farmer father makes in a month. And when she sends money back to the family then her working in a bar is never mentioned and everyone loves her just the same.

Here are some facts; The NBI (National Bureau of Investigations) which is equivalent to the American FBI is located on Taft Street in Manila. Within one block there are numerous night clubs that offer bar girls that you pick from the stage dancing, pay the bar fine and go and have sex. Everyone knows about it including the NBI who frequent the place. All of these establishments pay protection money to the police.

The EDSA International Entertainment Complex, known as the warehouse locally, located in Pasay in Manila is a huge warehouse that has 7 night clubs inside and has easily a 1000 prostitutes working on any given night. Every policeman knows about it and so many girls apply that they only pick the prettiest ones.

But I have to say prostitution will never be legalized because Filipinos want to save face to the outside world and act like it doesn't exist. Secondly, and probably more relevant, is that the Philippines gets USAID (197 million in 2012) based on a tier rating system. If they made prostitution legal they would be considered as having a bad human trafficking rating and lose USAID) so the Philippines conduct fake bar raids with USA government organizations (IJM) and round up a few bar girls once in a while to show the USA they are actively combating prostitution. Everyone knows is just for show.

Lastly, the Philippines are rooted in Catholicism and we all know the church will forgive the sinner but still will never support prostitution. So as long as the police turn a blind eye and the church will forgive you regardless of what you do coupled with USAID, why change things when it is working just fine? Everyone wins.

Have you been to any countries known for their large sex industries like Thailand or Costa Rica? What do you think about them?

I have been all over the world. You would be surprised at the large scale sex industry almost everywhere. Thailand alone has many large sex complexes like Nana Plaza, Patpong and Soi Cowboy. Pattaya which was just a crappy beach area until the US military open an R&R center there during the Vietnam war turning the town into one large sex haven where now the famous Walking Street is has thousands of sex workers.

There is red light district in Tokyo called Kabukicho that has well over 3,000 sex parlors. The streets are lined with porno shops, strip clubs, karaoke bars and the like. It is expensive, but there are thousands of prostitutes available. Beware; some clubs will not let foreigners inside.

One my favorite places to go is Naha City in Okinawa, Japan. There are many clubs and most refer to it as Soap Land. The whole area is filled with brothels. I would guess about 30 to 40 brothels with big signs and most have their prices on posters right on the street for everyone to see. There are night clubs everywhere and one place you have to go see is the "stage" where they have a strip show and then take someone from the audience, throw a condom on him and fuck him on stage.

In Amsterdam there is huge red light district called De Wallen which is a network of small alleyways that has hundreds of small rooms with big windows facing the alleyways. You just walk around and look in the window and pick the girl you want to have sex with. Many of these girls are married and this is a real job for them. I was not very impressed because they seemed to be too professional and business like. I prefer small petite Asians that at least act like they like you. Fucking in Amsterdam is like going to the store to buy milk. Boring.

One entertainment area I enjoy is in Kowloon, Hong Kong. Normally when I travel I try to make a layover in Hong Kong and head over to Portland Street where you can find hundreds of night clubs, massage parlors, hostess bars and just plain old brothels. All of them are filled with prostitutes. Prostitution is completely legal so you will find every ethnic group there. I have fucked white Canadians, Brazilians, and Africans there. Mostly the girls are from mainland China.

There is prostitution all over Asia but most are not in one large complex but are located singularly or in small enclaves covering a large area. The sex industry as a whole is massive.

What is the biggest inconvenience of making porn?
Worrying if you are going to be set up by the police.

If you had a friend or family member who wanted to get into the business, what would you tell them?
If you going to just be the stickman then it can be fun. But if you are stickman and producing it can be lots of work. I would tell them to forget about producing and just go have fun.

Has the rise of the internet made it easier or more difficult to find models? I hear that many women are now afraid of doing one off videos since they may be seen by someone they know.

Yes the internet is a huge obstacle for finding girls willing to get filmed. They all have heard stories about someone's picture on the internet. Sometimes I have to fuck 10 girls just to find one that is willing to get filmed (poor me...haha).

I don't think it is the internet as much as all these sites that steal your images/videos and then publish them all over the net. And believe me DMCA can't control very much as they do not have jurisdiction in most countries. It is the same as in the music industry where nobody buys CD's anymore. The only thing you can do is have exclusive content and have regular updates to stay ahead of the pirates.

Have you ever had to cancel a shoot because of something like a girl with an STD or a bad odor?

Funny you should ask. I have never had nor would I have sex with someone that had symptoms of a STD or any abnormality. But I did recently film a threesome and after fucking one girl for awhile her pussy reeked and the other girl held her nose and got off the bed and just watched.

I've asked this question to other producers, but how do you think porn can continue to be profitable with all of the free content now available online? Has the advent of file sharing, tube sites and the like put a big dent in your earnings?

It does erode the business model. I don't see a solution at present. As I mentioned, I just try to stay ahead of them by having exclusive content that no one else has and updating with new material regularly so that the pirates are always a step behind.

151

How long do you plan on producing porn?

When it stops becoming fun or profitable.

Do your friends and family know about your work? Do you have a significant other?

No.

What do you think about my site, if anything?

Looks good. Good luck.

Escort and Author Miranda Writes

Miranda Writes is pretty obviously a pen name. I have no problem with that. My birth certificate doesn't say "Rockit Reports" either. Free speech is fueled in many situations by anonymity.

Miranda Writes uses her experience as an escort to write books. In some ways she isn't all too different from me. She was willing to do the following interview that brings out some of her knowledge and ideas well.

How long have you been writing?

Since I was old enough to hold a pencil in my hand.

How much of what you write in this book is fact and how much is fiction?

100% of A Hooker's Variety Show is fact. 100%. Certain characteristics were changed in order to protect identities and generalities were used when specifics could cause potential safety issues. One has to balance the reality of the book with the reality she–and her friends and family–face in the real world.

What inspired you to write this book?

Writing was a great way to process my experiences. I laughed a lot.

Do you ever read trashy sites like mine? Perhaps I have outdated sexist attitudes but I'm often shocked by the

number of female readers. I've even noticed some similarities between you and I. You write about the reasons guys want to pay for action. I've done the same numerous times.

Not to go all Sarah Palin on you, but I read everything. Sure, I enjoy a "trashy" site once in a while, and I'm certainly interested in sex worker education and advocacy sites. But more often than not I'm reading hardcore news and hardcore literature, not hardcore sex. My greatest asset isn't my ass. It's my mind. And I make sure to feed that greedy bitch regularly with the stuff she needs to keep going.

How strict are you with the need for a reference? Some guys have written me saying they can't book sessions with escorts in their area because they're new to it all and all of the escorts ask for references.

I don't require references if other screening methodology can be utilized. As for what those methods are? You seem to be a nice guy, so let's not go there. I'd hate to have to kill ya.

What is the biggest misconception people have about escorts?

Where oh where to begin?

I guess we'll go with this...

Most think those who are educated, sober, and mentally and financially stable don't engage in sex work unless they are somehow forced into the situation. They're wrong. Many, many sex workers choose this way of life as their profession or as a dalliance. Sex workers span the educational, sociological, financial, political, religious, racial, cultural, and geographical spectrum. They represent all ages, all types of sexual identities, and all types of physicalities. You will somehow come into contact with one of us today, and you probably won't even

154

know it. Believe that. Take it to the bank. We do.

What is the biggest mistake guys make with escorts?

They don't treat them with the respect every human being deserves.

What's the worst experience you ever had in sex work? What's the best?

Ah. You'll just have to wait for future books!

When it comes to sex work are you for legalization, decriminalization or something else all together?

Decriminalization.

In a part of a book you go over some of the texts you've received. One guy asked if you'd gotten fatter then tried for a discount on the basis of that assumption. You responded by writing "I actually charge by the pound, so I charge more now." This made me laugh out loud. I'm always amazed by some of the things I hear from escorts and other sex workers. Or at least I was until I started to see some similar comments show up on this site. Thankfully they are few and far between. How often are you actually confronted with this kind of outrageous behavior?

Every. Single. Day.

If a friend or family member told you they wanted to get into the business what would you tell them?

Know your mission. Know your boundaries. Know your endgame. Know that your gut knows more than you ever will. Follow it. Always.

155

Some incredibly beautiful and intelligent escorts have told me that they've fallen for clients time and time again. This is actually one of the biggest complaints I hear about the work. Do you have any experience with that? What would you tell these escorts?

Actually, I've had the opposite experience. I entered into this industry because I wanted sex without the commitment. I've had more than one marriage proposal in two years. Believe that. But while I love my clients, I am "in love" with none of them. Nor have I ever been.

What would I tell another escort? Nothing, as that's exactly what my advice would be worth. Every person and situation is different.

What do you think of pornography? Would you ever get involved in that?

I have no issues with pornography and maybe, just maybe, enjoy some of it myself.

Would I get involved? I want to say no, but one should never say never.

What are you reading right now? What are some of your favorite books of all time?

I'm reading a couple of incredible books right now. *The Nazi Officer's Wife: How One Jewish Woman Survived the Holocaust* has bent my mind in all sorts of ways. Check it out. It's by Edith Hahn Beer and Susan Dworkin. *Lamb*, by Christopher Moore, is double-over-till-your-sides-ache-funny and tells the story of Christ from the perspective of his BFF, Biff.

Moby Dick is my favorite book of all time.

Thanks a lot for taking the time to do this interview. Other than your new book what else should we look out for?

Thanks for platform! Appreciated. The sequel to this one is already in the works. Also, there will be a fetish version coming out soon. For updates, or just to say "hey", follow me on Twitter @MsMirandaWrites.

Porn Star Mia Li

The number of Asian-American porn stars regularly performing in the US is limited. That is somewhat understandable considering that Asians are a minority in the country. Recently several Asian-American starlets have emerged alongside Asian women who have immigrated to the US.

Mia Li popped up on my radar when she first started doing porn. I was happy to see a new face and I reached out to her. She was gracious enough to do the interview that follows.

First let me ask all the usual questions: where are you from, how old are you and how did you get into porn?

I am from Queens, New York and am 24. Webcamming was my diving board into the porn industry.

Did you have any hesitation getting into porn now that the industry is making less money than it used to?

I had reservations due to the nature of the work and not the pay. As a cammer I am able to control my rates and manage to make a decent living.

I first saw you in a streaming Kink video online. You either greatly enjoyed it or you are a spectacular actress. Do you prefer Kink work to "vanilla" porn?

Honestly, I don't consume a lot of pornography. In regard to my preference of kink to vanilla sex, I like both equally. It all depends on the people with whom I'm having fun. I really feed off of the energy and preferences of my lovers.

What's your take on social media as it relates to porn?

I think social media, such as Twitter, makes it easier for fans to reach out and communicate with their favorite porn stars. The downside of social media is that privacy is growing less and less sacred.

Do you ever watch Japanese porn? What do you think of that?

I watched a few Japanese porns, particularly hentai. I am a huge fan of hentai porn because of how amazingly the voice acting and the animation pairs with each other.

On a normal non-porn day what kind of panties do you wear?

I wear exceptionally comfortable thongs or full back panties. Comfort is king when I'm not shooting porn.

What's your opinion of prostitution? Some porn stars are now openly selling sexual services to average Joes, especially in Japan and Europe. Would you ever consider escorting?

I think that individuals have a right to their body and if they want to sell sexual services that is their prerogative. I would never consider escorting because I would rather the lover and I to mutually come to the conclusion that we both want to fuck, rather than having it come to be because of an economical exchange. I love being a porn actress because it is a performance to create content for people to enjoy sexually.

What was the first porn you saw?

I think the first porn I saw was a soft core on pay per view.

What was your first sexual experience?

Masturbation when I was rather young. I don't think I quite knew that what I was doing was masturbation. All I knew was that it felt amazing.

Who is your favorite porn star?

I don't have a favorite porn star because I simply don't watch porn.

If a family member or friend wanted to get into porn and come to you for advice, what would you say?

Be extremely self aware of what you are willing to do and think the decision through thoroughly.

What do you think about the push to require condoms in porn?

I think it's an absurd infringement of our rights as sex workers and also a violation of already implemented safety protocols.

Are you often recognized in your day to day life?

Frankly, I am far too new to be recognized. I have been recognized just a handful of times.

Some people have said that stripping and working adult cam sites is now more profitable for women than doing porn scenes. Do you agree with that?

I don't have personal or anecdotal data on this opinion, so I can't say. In regard to camming, I know that on a good day I can make as much as I would on a normal porn shoot.

A lot of porn stars now have Amazon wish lists where fans can buy them things they like. You also have one. Have you gotten many things this way?

I have gotten quite a few things this way. I use my Amazon wish lists as a way for my fans to get to know me through the items and comments I post on them.

What is your favorite book? Your favorite movie?

My favorite book currently is The Windup Bird Chronicles by Murakami. I'm not certain of my favorite movie right now.

Thanks so much for taking the time to answer these questions. Where can readers find more info about you? Do you have a website?

Readers can follow me on Twitter or Instagram @LoveMiaLi. To check out my written work, I contribute to Kinky.com and have a blogger under the handle TheEuphemisticMinister.

Porn Star Marica Hase

Japanese porn, known locally as Adult Video or "AV", is huge. In the land of the rising sun huge sums are spent on producing and purchasing porn. With the spread of the internet came the spread of Japanese porn. Although it is produced for a local audience the quality is so high that others couldn't help but enjoy it.

Still Japanese porn producers and performers have only just begun to attempt to tap into external markets. A pioneer in this regard is Marica Hase who went from performing in Japanese AV to becoming a porn star in her own right in the United States. After working with major studios and even appearing in some of the most well known adult magazines in the country she agreed to do the question and answer session that follows.

Let's start with the basics. How old are you and where are you from?

I am a Lolita MILF, haha. I moved here in USA from Tokyo of Japan last year.

Do you have a boyfriend?

No, I don't have any boyfriend.

When did you first have sex?

When I am high school student.

When did you see your first porn movie?

I often bought porn movies after I become 20 years old, but I skipped the sex scenes. I love looking at cute or beautiful girls, and just enjoyed watching them strip and tease.

How did you get into porn in Japan?

The biggest porn production company held a huge audition to find the next girl to win the exclusive contract with them. They advertised that the winner would get many deals with big TV shows, magazines, radios, silent movies and porn "if you become next our exclusive girl".

I had been already modeling non-adult since I was 20 years old. I really loved acting in the front of camera, so I wanted the challenged and won.

How long did you do porn in Japan before coming to the US to do it?

About 5 years.

Did you visit the US before deciding to do porn there?

Yes. I came here once before I decided to do porn here, to interview agents and to learn about American shoots.

Did you have sex with any guys who weren't Japanese before doing porn?

No, I didn't.

I think you have won some awards for your work in the US. Are you now more well known in Japan or America?

I am a Penthouse Pet of USA, and I have been nominated for multiple awards like AVN, Xbiz, Sexiest Awards, but I haven't actually won any award in the US sadly. For DDF Awards in Europe, I was a runner-up, and I have won many Japanese awards in the past.

I think most of Japanese porn watchers know me and follow me. Some have watched me since I started in modeling in Japan, and others took up interest for becoming the first the Penthouse Pet of America and relocated here to work. So I have more Japanese fans, but American fans are increasing.

How did you feel about shooting porn in the US? In Japan I think you are paid more and have dedicated teams of makeup assistants. In the US things are more casual but I've heard they can be more fun.

That's exactly right.

There are many cultural differences between the Easterners and the Westerners. Everything is different form Japan; makeup, shooting style, the way you smile or pose, pay scale and the way people think about sex.

I really enjoy working in both USA and Japan. I love adventures... I always look for something new when I'm in the front of camera.

Do you prefer to watch American or Japanese porn?

I enjoy both. I don't care which country they are from. What is important is how talented the cast is.

Why aren't there more foreigners in Japanese porn?

Almost of all big Japanese companies have the policy that forbids foreign models. Only few small Japanese companies will hire them.

What do you think about *fuzoku* in Japan?

I don't have any problem with anyone who works in fuzoku. If they're proud of what they do, good for them.

How about bukkake?

I love bukkake. It's a traditional Japanese porn fetish act. I love being submissive, because I am an authentic Japanese porn star. It feels like a dream.

Japanese porn is popular on many websites in the US but most people don't know the names of porn stars except for some like you and maybe Maria Ozawa. Why do you think that is?

There are many reasons, but the biggest one is because of the mosaics. In Japan, they have to hide the genitalia in the videos by law so they apply the mosaic effect on the screen. Because of this, the men got used to fantasizing about what the pussies actually look like during the sex acts. If a girl appear in a foreign porn and reveal her pussy to the world, it would be very difficult for her to go back and work in the Japanese porn industry unless she is already a huge star. The major porn makers will no longer book them. That's why very few models would try working for non-Japanese porn makers.

Your English is pretty good. Has it improved since you started doing porn in the US?

Thank you. I took me only one day to decide to come to US to do porn, so I didn't study English before I came here.

I am learning English from my every day activities in

the US like working, chatting with my America fans, hanging out my America friends and my roommate.

Are you often recognized outside? What do you think of your fans?

In Japan yes. I couldn't walk outside without a hat or pair of shades by myself. I just worked a lot because I enjoyed the work, then people started recognizing me. I never thought about becoming famous or thought of myself as a "star". I really appreciate my fans, but I feel awkwardly bashful when they treat me like a star.

You've done a lot of great scenes. Some show you doing things like anal and squirting. Is there anything you haven't tried that you still want to do?

I think I have already tired just about every kind of sex act, but the great think about porn is that every day is a new challenge with different co-star and scripts. I want to do many more scenes.

What is your favorite food? Your favorite drink?

I started to work out so I can get better at pole dancing. I need to build more muscles, so my current favorite drink is Muscle Milk Protein with soy milk, hee-hee! What's great about me is that I can enjoy just about every kind of food.

How long will you continue to do porn? What are your future plans?

I want to continue to be in the porn or the related industries as long as I can. In addition to being in the porn shoot as a model, I am discussing several projects including publishing my autobiography, producing porn as well as appearing in regular (non-adult) American TV shows.

The Japanese porn industry treats girls as expendables. As the internet became the mainstream, less and less porn is sold as DVD, and girls could survive the industry for 3 years at the most today.

In America, those girls who succeed in becoming famous in porn can find many ways to make money, and the amount of money the Americans are willing to afford on entertainment is astronomically much more than Japan… it is really the land of opportunity.

I want to take on a wide variety of work in the American entertainment industry as the first international porn star from Japan, a frontier who showed new possibilities to the small Japanese porn industry. I hope my name will appear and remain in the text book for porn history long after I retire.

What advice do you have for people who want to do porn?

Don't be a porn star. Haha.

Porn is a lot harder work than it looks. There are only a handful of people who become successful. Once you appear in porn, you will be discriminated against in many occasions. If you want "an easy" job, you are better off staying away from porn, however, if you have guts and want to give it all you got with your head held high, it can turn out to be a hundred times more rewarding than doing "normal" work.

Thanks so much for doing this interview. Where can readers go to find out more about you?

Marica-hase.com is my website!

Porn Star Nasse Laila

Porn is big in Germany. In the rest of the world, German porn has developed a reputation for being very hardcore. Nasse Laila isn't necessarily a part of the organized German porn scene, but she is still very interesting.

Known as "Germany's Hottest Cum Face," she has gained some level of prominence and fame on the internet through her self-produced porn scenes.

Her fame hasn't gone to her head however. She is still very down to earth as illustrated in this interview and her maintenance of a "regular job" in the insurance industry.

How old are you and where are you from?

I´m 23 years old and live in Berlin, Germany.

What was your first sexual experience?

Hmm I would say the boring fuck called the first one.

When did you first watch porn?

I think I was thirteen when I first watched a porn video.

How did you get into making porn?

I like to be watched while having sex and it makes me horny to know that someone faps while watching me so I decided to make some pictures and videos. I got lots of good feedback so I never stopped do it since this day.

How did you come to specialize in cum? Was that something you liked before you started making movies?

Even before I started making movies I liked to have cum on my face. Now I love it. It gives me a good feeling to get covered with cum after a nice fuck. Nothing shows me better that the guy is totally satisfied than a huge load of cum in my face.

Do you prefer facials or creampies?

I like both but I prefer facials. Sure it´s a nice feeling to get my pussy filled up with jizz but a huge shot all over my face satisfies me even more.

You're billed as "Germany's hottest cumface" in English and "Princess of Facials" in German. Do you ever work outside of Germany? Do most of your viewers come from Germany or other countries?

I've never worked outside of Germany. I have a regular work as a secretary in an insurance office. My videos are my little slutty hobby that helps me to relax after a hard day of work.

Most of my viewers are from Germany but I have a little fan base in the US and I like them very much.

What is your private sex life like?

I love sex and I am not only doing it in front of a camera. But what you get to see from me on video is what you can expect from me in my private sex life.

Do you ever have sex with strangers?

Yes when I was nineteen I had a date with two strangers and it turned into a hot threesome but today I prefer to have sex with people I know because the world is dangerous for such a tiny girl like me.

Do your friends or family know what you do?

Not all but those who do know have accepted it so everything is cool.

What do you think about prostitution?

It's something I never would do but it's nothing bad and we should be glad that it exists.

What advice would you have for someone who wanted to follow in your footsteps? Would the advice change if a family member asked?

My first advice would be: "Don't do it for the money. Do it because you like it." It will be the same for any family member.

When was the last time you had sex?

You really want to know this? Haha. Okay, it was about 3 hours ago.

What kind of things do you like to do when you're not having sex?

I play guitar, go out with friends and I love to play on my PS4. Yes I'm a so-called gamer girl.

What is your favorite website?

Hm, I would say it´s eBay. I don't know why but if I search for something my first place to look will be eBay.

Thanks for doing this interview. Where can readers find out more about you?

Visit my homepage Nasse-laila.tv

Japanese "Delivery Health" Worker

Delivery Health, or delihel, is a type of sex work done in Japan. Delivery Health services send women out to meet customers for adult activities like hand jobs and blow jobs Although full sex is prohibited both by Japanese law and delihel policy it still occurs at times.

In a past volume of *Sex Talk,* I published translations of two interviews with guys who manage delihel agencies that first appeared on the infamous Japanese website 2Chan. Below, I publish an interview with a delivery health worker that I did myself.

When I do an interview I always start off by asking for age and origin. So where are you from and how old are you?

I am twenty-seven. I'm from northern Japan.

Are you really twenty-seven? You look so much younger. People often say that to Asian women but I actually mean it. I would have guessed you were in your early twenties.

You are too kind!

How did you get into this line of work?

Well… I wanted to gain real massage skills but I also wanted to make good money.

And how did you find your current job?

Google.

Wow! I guess you really can find anything with Google nowadays.

Yes. It was easy.

Why did you choose to work at your current employer rather than another company?

They offered the best money and they work with foreigners. Personally I prefer foreigners to Japanese guys for customers. I also get to practice speaking English.

Do you have a boyfriend?

No. Because of my work. I don't think guys would understand it or accept it.

It is interesting to hear you say that you prefer foreigners when so many adult shops in Japan forbid them. Would you date a Japanese guy?

Sure.

Would you date a foreigner?

I would date a foreigner too. I don't care about that so much when it comes to dating. I worked a regular job abroad in an English-speaking country and I met a lot of great guys. I hope to go back some day.

Is this your first time working in the adult entertainment industry?

Yes it is.

So did you have to do any kind of training before you started?

Yes. I got a lesson in massage from one of the other women who has been working for a while. She showed me how to give massages and explained how the sessions should go.

Did she just explain things or did she show you?

She showed me. She massaged another one of the ladies like a customer. I watched and learned a lot. Now I have my own style.

Were you nervous the first time you had an appointment with a customer?

No not really. As I said I have known foreigners before. It was exciting. Not scary.

Does your family know about your work?

No they don't.

What do you think they would do if they found out?

Do? Do?? They would cry!

Have you had any bad experiences since you started working?

Not really.

I'm pleasantly surprised to hear that no customers tried to push you to do more than the regular services your shop offers.

A few did try. But when I told them stop one time they stopped. They didn't push at all.

So you have been happy with your experiences in this line of work?

So far all of the guys have been cool. Very kind guys!

What is the best thing about doing this kind of work?

When customers say thank you after a session. I really feel like I did a good job and made them happy.

And what is the worst part?

Worst part? Hmm. I guess if there a slow day and there isn't much to do.

Is this the best job you have ever had?

Yes it is.

So it sounds as if you like the work. Do you plan on doing it for a while?

I don't plan to do this work for more than a year.

Do you watch porno?

Yes I do.

Are you just saying that because it is what guys want to hear?

No. I do watch it on my own time. I like it. Maybe I am strange for a woman.

Do you prefer Western porn or Japanese adult video?

I like them both.

What do you think about the kinds of guys who call shops like yours for sexual services?

I understand them. I don't think anything about them really. Before I would wonder what kind of guys would spend money for these things. Now I get it. They just want good feelings. I really want them to enjoy Japan so I give them my best.

Thanks for taking the time to talk to me. I know that people will be interested in your thoughts.

My pleasure.

Chinese Porn Starlet

The following interview was done with an adult webcam model and amateur porn star who started posting her videos for sale online. She quickly became very popular thanks in large part to her good looks. Soon after agreeing to do this interview however she apparently ran into some trouble and removed her work from the web. The interview she did gives insight into her thoughts not long after getting into the game. We can only guess what she thinks today.

First I want to say that I think you're very attractive and you make great videos. Good job! How old are you? Where are you from?

I am 22 sexy years old. I come from the southern part of China, near Shanghai.

How and when did you start making porn clips?

I started making my own porn clips when I was 18, mainly just for fun, but I never did anything with them. Then the middle of last year I started posting some on various websites.

Who is the lucky guy in your videos?

He is my boyfriend, he helps me with everything and is really supportive.

Do you use any outlets other than ManyVids to make money with adult entertainment? Do you broadcast on adult

webcam sites?

I was broadcasting on Chaturbate before and someone recorded my cam show and posted it around, so I don't know if I will use it again or not. I have also used Extra Lunch Money which was decent, but not as good as Many Vids in terms of sales.

Where are you most popular? Is there any particular place where a lot of your customers seem to come from?

I think I am most popular on Manyvids (I've gone from being rated around number 2000 something to girl number 30 within two months. I'll be in the top 10 within another two months or I'll cry. Reddit and Twitter. I am recently playing with Tumblr which I have high expectations for as I'm starting to get a following there too!

Are your porn clips your main source of income or just a side job?

I have a part time job as a language teacher. So I guess they are both part time jobs, although they earn me about the same about per month so far.

Do you have any plans to pursue porn further as time goes on?

I am undecided yet. I am happy with how I am doing things at the moment so lets let fate decide that one.

Do you watch porn yourself?

Yeah I actually do, which is pretty unique for Chinese girls. Porn is 'illegal' here, although its everywhere. One of my favorite websites would be Pornhub, mainly I like watching blonde girls with white guys, banging hard.

Yeah, porn is illegal in countries like China and South Korea. What do you think about that?

I think porn being illegal is a joke, because its readily available in both of those countries. Most people in China and Korea watch Japanese porn though, its interesting how different true 'Asian' porn is from 'Western' porn in terms of style and what people enjoy.

A lot of Asian porn is pretty in line with Asian culture where the girls aren't the aggressors and are kinda resistant to having sex which is exactly what Asian culture is like because all Asian girls have to pretend to be 'pure' and not want sex, even though we like sex as much if not more than Western girls — look at how many Chinese people there are.

Do you think that China will ever have its own porn industry?

I think it will take another 20 years. China is changing incredibly fast and taking on a lot of Western culture, but there are still very strong morals against porn and being open sexually (although everyone here is banging a lot).

It would be pretty cool though.

Do your family and friends know about your video work?

Uh, hopefully not. It's unlikely they will find out due to the great firewall.

Are you ever recognized in your daily life by people who have watched your videos?

Yeah I have once. About a month or so ago a foreign guy came up to me on the street and called me by my online alias which was a little scary. I didn't expect that, so I just pretended I wasn't me and ran away. I was pretty nervous about the experience as it's the first time I've been recognized ever.

Have you or would you ever date a fan?

I haven't dated any fans yet but I am open to it. It just depends on if I currently have a boyfriend or not. I currently do but he isn't always in the same city as me, so my fans still have hope.

What do you think is the best clip you've made so far?

This is a really really hard question to answer. I probably can't list one. My sexuality came through really well in the jack of instruction video I did with sperm in my mouth. My perfect blowjob video came out very well thanks to a great camera, lighting and lots of angels. My school girl doggy style video was of course incredibly hot because I was wearing a school girl outfit.

The clips that turn out the best always do so because I am really getting into it at that particular point.

If you could make any sort of porn clip what would it include?

I would love to have a scene where it's me, a guy and three or four other girls in a beautifully furnished room with a couch, a bed, a dining table (with candle sticks) and a fireplace, drinking red wine, eating nice French food, then as we drink more everyone starts to dance, you can feel the seductive rhythm of the music and feel the warm flush of the beautiful French red wine as it slides down your throat.

The scene plays out where we have a handsome guy playing a guitar or some sort of instrument (which is where the music comes from) and the girls are all eating and drinking, we drink enough to get to the point where we whisper to each other and come up with the idea of sitting at the musicians feet.

From there things get hot as we all start touching him and rip his pants off, and well you can imagine the rest.

We all end up naked, licking red wine off each other and banging each other everywhere.

How often do you make new videos?

I try to make a new video or two every week. It really just depends though. Sometimes life happens and I don't get one done for a few weeks.

I also like to wait for inspiration so I take videos that I also really like watching and masturbating too.

What are your goals for the future?

Uh, probably my own website. From what I've learned during the last year I think that's the way to go as you have more control over everything.

Other than that, I wanna travel overseas, explore the world, maybe hook up with some girls. Actually I recently have been thinking how could I get myself into a situation that involves me and four or five other girls all naked and making each other squirm... still haven't quite figured that out yet though.

You seem to have no problem with cum. You can take it on your face or in your mouth without issue. When were you first exposed to semen? What do you think of women who are grossed out by cum?

Yeah. This is actually because of my current boyfriend. He likes putting it on my face, in my mouth, on my back, seeing me swallow it, on my chest, on my ass.

So exposed isn't a very specific word. I could say I saw it in porn before I actually had sex, but my first time being actually exposed to it was my first bf when I was 16. I didn't take it in my mouth or on my face until I was around 20 though. I regret wasting the 4 years of not doing it, because it feels good. Liquid love.

I think women who are grossed out by sperm need to loosen up and become more accepting of their own sexuality. Taking cum in my mouth definitely makes my bf love me more, swallowing more so.

What are your favorite and least favorite sex acts?

My favorite thing to do during sex would be giving "air pressure" blow jobs In case you don't know, those are when you suck the guys cock to make it hard, then make it super wet with saliva and then loosely suck it by moving up and down it the same you would if trying to suck wet ice cream up. This creates friction because the air is moving through the liquid and there's a "drinking soup" sorta sound.

There has to be enough of a gap for air to move through when you suck.

My personal record doing this is making my bf orgasm in 49 seconds.

My other favorite sexual act is definitely squirting. My bf trained me how to squirt and now it happens an amazing amount.

My least favorite is being told to say degrading things about myself. I had this experience once and I didn't like it, so I won't do it again.

Have you ever had group sex?

Not yet.

What's the kinkiest thing you have ever done?

I once got fucked with an ice dildo, a hot towel dildo and my boyfriend's cock all at the same time. It was incredibly intense. I even wrote a story about it.

My boyfriend prepared a huge ice dildo, the hot towel thingy, laid me down and proceed to destroy me with them. It was an incredibly rewarding experience. Not what I expected at all, having the huge ice dildo inside me and my boyfriend's cock or the hot towel inside me at the same time was incredibly kinky.

Which sexually situations that you've been in have turned you on and off the most?

I remember the wettest I've ever been was the first time my boyfriend put his hand on my throat while making love with me. I was on my back and he pinned me with his big hand around my little neck and banged me really hard. It still makes me wet now just thinking about it.

The most turned off I've ever been was one time when I went on a date with some Italian guy and he tried to make me give him a blowjob in the taxi. That date finished quickly, with no blowjob.

I have met a bunch of very nice Italians since then though.

What do you think about women selling used panties online?

I think it's an interesting way to make money. I am curious what the guys actually do with the panties.

I personally haven't sold any panties online as of yet but am open to it.

What do you think about prostitution?

It's the oldest job in the world. I don't think its a bad thing, just so long as people aren't getting hurt. I don't see myself getting into that industry any time soon, unless someone is going to throw me about $100,000 USD. Haha.

What was the last movie you watched? How was it?

The last movie I watched was Big Hero 6 with that big white thing. In Chinese its called 'Big White' and I like it. I even won a toy of it which I have at home somewhere.

I liked the movie because it has a lot of fun scenes and the big white is very cute. I would like to own one, so if any robotics nerds see this and wanna invent one for me, I'll appreciate it.

Porn Star Aubrey Gold

Aubrey Gold could very accurately be described as an "All-American Porn Star." She has blond hair and the kind of looks that fans came to expect when video porn was having its heyday in the 1990's.

I reached out to her not long after seeing her pop up in a porn I was watching, uh, purely for research purposes. She was gracious enough to do the interview that follows.

How old are you and where are you from?

I'm 18, from Alabama.

How old were you when you lost your virginity?

I was 14.

How old were you when you saw porn for the first time?

I was 12.

How did you get into porn?

I knew a guy from Lakeland, Florida who knew my first agent in Ft. Lauderdale, Florida.

Do you still watch porn now that you make it yourself?

Yes I still watch porn a lot. Everyday mostly haha.

There's no denying that you're a very attractive woman. That isn't always the case with what I see. How much do you think looks matter in the American porn industry today?

Looks in porn matter to an extent. You can't be cute and not know how to fuck. Just have a certain look or style if you're not cute and if you're cute great. It's more about personality .

A lot of people say porn is dead. Is it? There are still lots of scenes coming out so there must be some money to be made!

I think porn won't die out. There's so much more things to do with it and technology! And I feel companies are starting to bring old school porn back.

Many women in the porn industry do feature dancing and other side gigs to make money. Do you get into any of that?

No, I haven't done featured dancing but I will! Haha.

Are you ever recognized by people when you're out in the street?

I've had people recognize me and follow me and stuff it's weird but cool sometimes, haha.

Do you have a boyfriend?

No boyfriend!

Have you or would you ever date a fan?

I might date a fan. I'd date whoever I like.

Do your family and friends know about your work?

Yes, my family knows.

What are the best and worst things about doing porn?

Good things are the money, acting, production, being my self, networking, traveling, sex, exploring, making something of myself, growing up on my own. Bad things shady people, drugs, problems if you're not smart and spend money!

What advice do you have to people who want to get into porn themselves?

Be very very smart and expand your mind and money to new things! Make an empire of different jobs. Be successful.

Do you think you make more or less doing porn than you would in the "mainstream" world?

More money in porn, but I'm going to work normally too!

How long do you plan on doing porn?

I forever love porn!

What's your favorite sex act?

I love head and foreplay and teasing the most about sex and dressing up as a different character.

What do you think about prostitution?

I don't care if you're a prostitute do what you want! Technically porn is the same except you make movies and something out of it.

Thanks so much for answering these questions. Where can readers see more of you?

Aubreygold.com and on Twitter @aubreygoldxxx.

Cam Model and Porn Star Crystal Clark

Several of the subjects that appear in the pages of Sex Talk prove just how big adult webcams have become. The webcam models I have interviewed have done everything from making a very good living as webcam models to getting into porn and even opening porn studios and becoming known all around the world for their work.

Crystal Clark is an American webcam model who has parlayed her popularity into more with the production of her porn scenes that she sells to eager fans from all over. Here is what she had to say about her life and her work.

How old are you?
Twenty-five.

How old were you when you lost your virginity?
Eighteen.

How old were you when you saw porn for the first time?
Ten.

How about adult webcams?
Haha. What about webcams? Hahaha. I love webcamming I think it's a great way to interact with fans, people face to face in a way. I enjoy viewing those watching me cams. So I know who

I am talking too.

How did you get involved in camming yourself?

I was looking for a new outlet to try. I am always looking for new things to adventure into.

Do you still watch porn or cams now that you make videos and broadcast yourself?

I still watch porn. Hahahaha. I love it. I watch a lot of the opposite to what I shoot. I love watching interracial porn and anal. I haven't ventured into either but I enjoy in my personal life so it's great to watch. I'm a big fan of blacked.com and tushy.com.

I film a lot of fetish and I do watch fetish porn because I have a lot of kinks, but now that I do so much of specific genres it's hard to get into other people's product of the same genre. Only because I'm a knit picker if it's something I know a lot about. Hahahaha

You're obviously an attractive woman. How much do looks matter in this industry? Are you doing well with your webcam career?

Oh thank you! That means a lot! Um, I would say yes and no. Sometimes it's all about the brains.

Some people say porn is dead. It's still coming out so it must make some money but I understand what they're saying. Cam sites seem to be all the rage and they're generating a lot of hype and income. Since that's the case why do so many cam models do videos too?

Well you need both really. You can only make so much *only*

190

camming and you can only make so much *only* making video. So best to do both. I don't think porn is dead at all. I just think people have discovered other types of porn but also piracy is really hurting the industry. That needs to stop.

You have your own website and a Clips4sale page. Are they popular?

I have two clip stores and they are I think? Haha. Both my stores are in top 50 categories in different fetish genres. So I think that's popular? My website meh, not so much. My current site is free for people to view pics and get links. I do have a pay site but it's not very active as I have more fun with my clips4sales. I love that company!

Do they generate more or less than your cam broadcasts?

Oh yeah my clip stores are my main source of income.

Are you ever recognized by people when you're out in the real world?

Haha. Sometimes! It's cool! But a lot of the time I notice men staring at me wondering who I might be. Where they have seen me… then they remember and shut down. Hahaha. I've filmed some pretty interesting kinks! Hahaha.

Any issues with creepers or stalkers? That's always seems like a possibility in this age of social media and Google.

Haha. Not yet! Hahaha. I'm friendly and invite people to come meet me around my city all the time so if I had stalkers I guess I haven't noticed because I love interacting with fans

Have you or would you ever date a fan?

191

Meh, if he was cool maybe? Haha. That's a silly question. Hahaha. It shouldn't matter if someone is a fan. If the connection is there the connection is there.

Do you have a boyfriend?

Nope.

Do your family and friends know about your work?

Some do and don't like it. Others do and think its awesome.

What's the best thing about doing adult cam shows?

Meeting new people!

What's the worst?

Long hours sometimes of empty rooms. Hahahaha.

What advice do you have to people who want to get into camming or selling porn videos online?

Be smart! Remember you are your own boss. So be smart!

Would the advice change if it was a family member asking?

Yeah. I would give them all the secrets.

Which adult cam site do you think is the best for broadcasters? Which is the best for viewers?

Myfreecams hands down but Camsoda is getting up there.

How often do you do cam shows? How often to put out new videos?

Cam shows when I'm home and not traveling two to three times a week. Video updates every other day sometimes every day.

Do you think you make more or less in your current line of work than you would in the "mainstream" world?

You mean mainstream world acting or like normal life? SAG rates… mainstream acting hands down makes more I think if you work enough or land a huge role. But normal job, no way! I make way more doing what I do that working a minimum wage job I would hate. Been there done that.

How long do you think you'll be camming?

I want to stop when I turn thirty.

What kind of panties are you wearing right now?

Haha. None.

Spit or swallow?

Depends on the taste.

Porn Star Cindy Starfall

An interview with Marcia Hase appeared earlier in this book. While she made her way from the Japanese porn industry to the American scene, the subject of this industry made what is arguably a much bigger jump.

Cindy Starfall went from being a regular Vietnamese girl to an American porn sensation. Once in the US she started performing on camera and the rest is history. She is now one of the more popular porn starlets in the country.

I'm sure you've been asked this countless times but could you tell us how and when you got into porn?

Growing up in an Asian culture, I was raised to please everyone. One day, I realized that I can't live my life trying to make people happy and I need to start thinking for myself. I enjoyed web camming and swinging with married couples and I realized that I'm a more sexual person than I thought. I was desperate in my corporate job. Everyone was very conservative. I wanted to work in a environment in which I could be myself. Being as sexual, energetic, and friendly as I am, adult film is a perfect fit for me. It has by far been the longest job I've ever held.

You said that you're Vietnamese in a scene that you did. How long ago did you come to the US?

My family immigrated from Vietnam ten years before me. I stayed with my nanny in Vietnam and I came to the US on a study abroad program when I was fifteen years old.

Are you more comfortable speaking in English or Vietnamese?

It depends on the situation. I like practicing and speaking English but I don't want to forget my roots so I still speak Vietnamese at restaurants or nail salons.

I think porn is illegal in Vietnam but if one looks, there are countless amateur sex videos made by Vietnamese people and uploaded to the internet. What do you think about that? Do you think any one knows about your porn work in Vietnam?

As I remember, when I lived there, porn was a very hush-hush issue. There wasn't much online porn access nor many nude magazines available. They mostly read about porn and sexual stories from comic books. I honestly don't see anything wrong with porn. I would love to shoot porn in Vietnam and would love to see Vietnamese girls embrace their sexuality.

Has porn changed since you first go into the industry?

Yes, there is way more free porn out now which makes the industry struggle. Because every porn video is available for free, consumers constantly want something new, something crazier. It's not about the pornstar anymore. It's more about what is the craziest video out there.

If you could start over again, would you still have made porn?

Absolutely! I love my job. I love sex and I love the fun environment when I'm at work.

When did you watch your first porn? Do you remember it?

I usually don't watch my porn. The first time I watched it was when I got nominated for the AVN awards and my porn was playing on the big screen. I was shocked and didn't recognize the girl on screen. I said to myself, "Wow, she looks so pretty with all that cum on her face"

What's your best sexual memory? What's your worst?

Best sexual memory has to be the 8-guy-gangbang scene in the movie "Starfall" (with Marica Hase). I felt like a piece of meat and that's what I want! All the guys surrounded me and gave me a great pounding. My worst memory is when I puked on camera during my first deep throat movie. No more orange juice before BJ scenes ever again!

When did you give your first blowjob? How was it?

My first blowjob was at a swinger party. I was curious with everything and I gave a blowjob to someone's husband while his wife took pictures. It was awesome! I loved looking up at his face to see how much he loved it. I love pleasing men.

If you had all the money you could ever want or need, would you still have done porn?

Yes and no. Yes a part of me will always be a performer but I would invest that money to do more behind-the-scenes things in the adult business. Either way, I'll always be in sex industry.

Have you had any issues with family or friends finding out about your porn work? Has it caused any problems in your personal life?

Yes, my mom recently found out about what I do. She was crying because she couldn't believe I actually love my job. She thought there was so many careers I could've done with my college degrees. I didn't expect my family to understand why I'm in porn. My mom and I have fell apart since then. I expected my family to disown me when they found out. I just wished they could've been happy for me, but that's just how Asian families are. In the end I would rather be happy and do what I love than do a job that makes others happy but not me.

What advice would you give someone who wanted to get into porn? Would the advice be any different to a stranger than it would be to a sister or close friend?

Do some research. Know the limit of what you want to do and what you don't. Choose a reputable agency. Save your money and invest. *Don't* let porn change who you are.

Who do you think is the best looking Vietnamese celebrity? The best looking celebrity in general?

She is half Vietnamese. She is still pretty in my book. Maggie Q.

What do you think about prostitution? How about the huge prostitution scene in Vietnam that operates under the radar in places like caphe om, karaoke om and massage parlors?

Just as my opinion on porn, I encourage women to embrace their sexuality. Get the money as a stepping stone to something bigger. However, I discourage forced prostitution. I am complete against women being forced or tricked into the industry by empty promises.

Have you ever tried stripping or adult webcamming? How was it?

I did webcamming before on Streamate, Live Jasmin, etc. However it wasn't for me because everyday was the same. I love porn much more because I get to play a different character everyday. I only take private webcam appointments now on Cindystarfall.net.

I never stripped before porn. Now I enjoy performing feature shows in various US cities. You can see when I'm coming to a town near you on my calendar on my website.

Are you ever recognized in the street?

Yes, plenty of times. I take pictures with them. Don't ever be afraid of talk to me. I love my fans.

Do you think the average porn star makes more or less money over their career than they would have if they done a "regular" job instead?

Adult industry salaries fluctuate. There will be a month when you are really busy and a month when you're not. I always save my money for rainy days. Porn isn't for everyone. You have to really love it to make a good living at it.

What kind of panties are you wearing right now?

Nothing. I don't wear panties off camera. When I do on camera, they come off in 2 seconds, which is perfect!

Do you ever have sex with random guys?

Of course. I love the thrill but I always use protection.

Prostitute Norma Jean

Norma Jean is a professional sex worker who plies her trade in one of the Nevada counties where it is legal. As many know these counties are the only places the sale of sexual services are legal in the United States.

The Bunny Ranch is probably the most well known legal brothel in the United States and that is where Norma Jean rose to prominence. In the age of social media and reality TV these sorts of things can happen. So, without further adieu, here is my interview with one of America's most famous sex workers.

Where are you from and if I may ask how old are you?

I am 36 years old. I was born in Great Falls, MT. But grew up as a teenager and spent most of my adult years in Seattle, WA.

Considering the nature of this site and your work there's no sense beating around the bush. How old were you the first time you had sex?

Haha. I was 14 years old. I was early at everything I guess sex too.

Where do you work and what kind of work do you do?

I am a legal working girl "prostitute". I work for the one and only "Dennis Hof". I float around from the World famous Bunny Ranch, to the Love Ranch Vegas, and to the Alien Cathouse. I do appointments at all 3 of the houses.

How did you get into that line of work and how long have you been doing it?

I started in the sex industry as a stripper at 19 and realized stripping wasn't my hustle, to cut throat and too much work for the return. So I found a path through a friend in escorting at 20 years old. I found brothels in the early 2000's and been working ever since. I've taken this career by the horns and fell I'm not a for now working girl, rather I am a career prostitute like so many successful others like Airforce Amy, Caressa Kisses, and Candy McKarthy.

You are obviously an attractive lady. How much of a role do looks play in the kind of work you do?

Looks is fifty percent of my business. Attitude and confidence is the other fifty percent. Don't get me wrong looks get me a call back faster when applying at a brothel, haha. I remember when I applied at the Bunny Ranch, I sent pictures in and within 48 hours I got a call to come in. I was hired as long as I could pass medical. "No problem" and get a sheriff's card and pass the background check "again, no problem." When I arrived to the Bunny Ranch talking to other bunnies I learned some waited 3 months or so to get hired and put on the schedule. So the point of my story is yes! Looks are a plus in this business. But I have seen Beautiful woman fail in this business over an entitled crappy attitude.

Have you ever refused a client for any reason?

I have refused a client or two in my time for having a dirty D.C. A D.C is what's known in brothel lingo as a dick check. Which is performed before any money can be expected. We are trained to look for legions, bumps, redness, discoloration, and common STDs. A diaper wipe soaked in alcohol is rubbed gently from the bottom of the scrotum to the tip of the head. If there is any legions the gentleman will squirm and we have the judgment and right to say no or refuse service.

Do you ever refuse requests for things out of the normal?

I have never refused a request. I love sex and I feel I am a strong representation being in the business. I consider myself a try-sexual, I'll try it once. Safe, Sane, and Fun! Everything's on the table with me!

Why do you think prostitution is illegal in most of the United States? Why are strip clubs approved while brothels are not?

Prostitution is nothing new. I guarantee in all of our generations back we all have had a prostitute in the family, perhaps a few. It's the oldest profession in the book along with fishing for woman. I feel a deep connection within this business and a soul pull. I see the problems lying in the laps of networks that when showing a prostitute in a sitcom or a movie it shows the lowest forms of prostitution. Instead of showing the upper higher end of it. Greedy, in thinking that wouldn't bring viewers in. But I think HBO had it right when they brought Cathouse to a series. Unfortunately, not everybody gets HBO. But surely even with an antenna you get Fox, CBS, NBC, and ABC. Which is a no brainer but surely a Big Brother or a Bachelor or Bachelorette or any of the other real live house series speaks for it. Haha.

Until education is wanted on a fair level of our business, a good majority of people will always have the image of the worst in this business. And of course the hypocrites who show two faces are the ones that have hidden wants and desires, but are afraid of what people might say or think I know who I am and what I do and why I choose to do it. Strip clubs being legal and prostitution not is a no brainer to me. Strip clubs will never require a weekly medical test. There are higher risks in running brothels compared to strip clubs that only require an entertainer's license easily obtained, fingerprints in some counties, a couple poles and a stage with seating, a DJ booth and proper insurance and boom! A strip club is born. A brothel requires oversight from local, state, and federal government. The background checks are extensive. The weekly medical is anywhere from $60.00 to $80.00 a week. Which the results are then faxed to the sheriff's department who are the ones that clear us through the house. The steps involved in the weekly maintenance of a brothel is busy and by the books. If strippers do give head or a sex act in the club my first question would be did you pass medical this week? Sex is fun, but not worth dying over.

What do you think about the large legal commercial sex scenes in countries like Germany?

Honestly I am for woman's sex rights. Anytime any government wants to pull their head out and realize legalizing prostitution lowers crime, brings in revenue and promotes safe sex. I'm in!

What's the best thing about the Bunny Ranch in your view?

The best thing about working for Dennis Hof is the respect and understanding he gives all his ladies. We all come from different walks of life, and he has a way of uniting us not only as a team but as a dysfunctional family as many one. It doesn't matter how harsh opinions are I and others are always made to feel acceptance and a part of something much bigger than someone's opinion.

What can guys do to make their experience at the Ranch as good as possible?

I get asked the question often how does a woman or man coming into a ranch prepare. I say look online to the ranch you're interested in, read the ladies biography, watch videos of the ladies and figure out what you're looking for by preshopping before you come in. Email the ladies and tell them the experience and type of party you are looking for. So when you come in you're not feeling rushed and shy to pick someone in the lineup. Your wants and needs are expressed and the beautiful lady of your choice will know how to accommodate your party.

Do you watch porn? Have your or would you ever do it yourself?

I do watch porn. I love BDSM, lesbian, bondage, role play films and of course my own home movies.

You're a pretty public person. Do your friends and family know what you do?

My friends and family know what I do. I pay taxes and make an honest living. I don't need approval when I'm contributing to society, not taking off the backs of other tax payers.

If someone wanted to follow in your footsteps what would you tell them?

I wouldn't give advice to someone wanting to follow in my footsteps. It's a journey one must take on their own. For their own wants and reasons. Each individual is destined for their own path not one path the same as another.

Last but not least I have to ask, what kind of panties do you wear when you're not working?

I don't wear panties in my personal life. I am pierced down below and underwear seems to snap. At work I wear thongs.

Is there anything else you'd like to say?

You don't have to agree with what I do. But I will say for those who are part of the Christianity faith like myself, for those who look down on us, please make sure that when you go to church on Sunday that you tell J.C. "Jesus Christ" the ladies at the ranches say hello to Mary Magdalen and all the other naughty woman of the bible. Remember no judgment it will be Sunday.

Thank you so much for doing this. I'm really glad we could make it happen.

Thank you for taking the time to have me for this interview and for all you readers out there thank you for taking the time to find out a little bit more about Ms. Norma Jean!

Transgender Porn Star Jessy Dubai

In recent years there has been a move to be more accepting of transgender people in the US and some other countries. There has also been some real push back.

Along with this has come a rise in the popularity of transgender porn. A lot of people are searching for "trap" or "ladyboy" videos to masturbate too. Jessy Dubai features prominently in many of those videos. This is what one of the most well known transgender porn stars in the world had to say to me.

How old are you and where are you from?

I am 26-years-old and I'm from the beautiful country of Mexico.

When did you first have sex?

Oh wow... Straight to the point I see. I was 16 when I first had sex but I was 15 when I started experimenting with some of my classmates.

I'm not really up on the issues of transgender people. My exposure is basically limited to the ladyboys in Thailand where I have spent a lot of time. The word ladyboy may even be offensive though it has widespread usage there. What should I know?

Well me personally, I don't like the world lady-boy. I know some other girls don't like that name either. I want to be treated like a woman. I don't want to hear the words "boy" or "man" when people address me.

What did your friends and family think about your transformation?

I think my family always knew. When I was little I was so feminine that when I started transitioning my family just accepted and learned to live with it. It was a bit harder to get my dad on board but finally after a year he accepted that he had a new daughter.

What do they think about your chosen career?

It's a hard and very competitive career. But I want to make it clear that I didn't choose it. IT chose me. And I am happy with the way it has all turned out.

How did you get into porn?

The movie *Zack and Miri Make a Porno* put the idea in my head. I was 19. When I was 23, I was arguing with my boyfriend at the time abut the porn we were watching. I said, "I don't like this porn." He replied, "Well why don't you make your own?" So I did. I applied to work for Kink.com and other companies. Soon enough I got the call that changed my path in life.

How often do you watch porn now?

Haha. Because of the people I follow on social media, editing my videos, helping other performers with their content, researching, and many other reasons, I watch porn almost every day. I probably watch porn while masturbating, probably three out of ten times.

What kind of porn do you like?

I like a variety. I can watch anything: gay, straight, orgies, gaping, you name it. I'm open to watching any porn at least once. It's also a great way to do research. Haha.

A lot of people say porn is dead though I think there is still plenty of porn worth paying for. What do you think? Have you seen any major changes since you entered the industry?

It's hard to say as I've only been in the industry two years. But porn is definitely not dead. I think there is still a lot of money to be made in porn. I feel that if performers, producers, and fans united, they can keep this industry growing.

What kind of work did you dream of doing as a child?

Being an actress has always been my dream. That's one reason I've been okay with being an adult actress. We all start somewhere. I still want to cross over and fulfill my dream.

What are your thoughts on Caitlyn Jenner's public transformation?

I think it was the perfect time to do it. It gave the transsexual community a new platform to be noticed. I also think she proved that you are never too old to live your dream and that no matter how much you try to suppress your true feelings, sooner or latter the truth will come out, and when it does, you will be much happier. Just look at old pictures of Caitlyn before her transition and look at her now. She was always meant to be this beautiful woman

What do you think about prostitution?

That's a hard question to answer. I would for sure not want my daughter or my sister to resort to it for many reasons, but if they did, I would understand and wouldn't judge them because I know from personal experience how hard life can get sometimes. Sometimes we have to do what we have to do to survive. I also believe a person is free to do what they please with their body. We all prostitute ourselves in some degree. We use our looks or flirt to get something in return. It happens in the office, restaurants, schools. People thinking "Maybe if I flirt with the manager and fuck him, he'll give me a raise, a better position, or just some extra cash."

What advice would you have for someone who wanted to get into porn?

Be 110 percent sure of your decision. Porn will change your life. Think about the good, the bad, and the maybes. Keep in mind if it's hard for you to have a relation outside porn, it'll be much harder if you do porn. Porn also can help you to love yourself more. It can teach you to be comfortable in your own skin. Also, get the crazy fantasies of leading a porno lifestyle out of your head: parties, drugs, unprotected sex… At least if you actually want to make it somewhere in this industry. Those things will just keep you distracted, and you'll spend money instead of making it. Focus on making good content. Show up on time to your shoots, tell yourself you are *not* a diva, at least not yet, so don't behave like one. You have to be professional just like in any business. Be nice to whoever you work with. And if there is something you don't like, it's okay to speak up and let the company, producer, actor etc. know what's going on.

What advice would you have for a guy who is interested in transgender women?

If you think about it dating a TS could be like dating your feminine buddy.

Thanks so much for doing this. Is there anything else you would like to say?

Oh no sweetie, thank you for letting me do this. It was fun answering all these questions.

Porn Star Jillian Janson

Porn is more widespread than ever but there don't seem to be as many big porn stars today as there were in the 1990's. There are exceptions but the days of the Jenna Jamesons and Maria Ozawas seem to be over.

Still some women are clearly more popular than others. Jillian Janson has come up in the US and gained a lot of followers along the way. Here's what the blond hair blue eyed star had to say.

What is your stage name and where are you from?

Jillian Janson from Minneapolis, MN. I have lived in Los Angeles almost three years now.

What was your earliest sexual experience?

I remember a time when I was about 10, there was this boy a year younger that liked me so much and we always held hands on the playground. One day we decided to go to the junkyard in our neighborhood to play, and when we hid out in an abandoned tractor tire he started to get a little dirty with me. He took out his little penis and being the curious kid I was I played with it. I didn't know it was giving him arousal and I didn't get him to "finish" or anything.

When did you first see porn?

I started watching it while I was pretty young actually. I was around 12 when I began getting off to it. I used it more to learn first, before I realized how horny watching it made me.

How did you get into the industry?

I joined a website that was intended for women to express their sexuality to others called MyFreeCams. Although it took about a week to start, I understood the concept right away and within the first few days into it I was contacted by an adult agency for a nude modeling opportunity. I talked with the agency for hours to get to know them and sort out all the details. Not long after I had landed in California for the first time, I knew my life would change forever. I was offered a chance to become somebody and to make a difference in lives besides my own, so I jumped on the idea as soon as it was offered. I have gained so much confidence for myself emotionally, mentally, and physically!

What are the best and worst things about doing porn?

I absolutely love this industry and I admire all it has done to help me become an inspiring individual. I feel comfortable in my own skin whether I'm 145 pounds or 110 with dark hair or blond. Everyone on set and those watching on screen have allowed me to express myself and my best qualities. I know that I stay safe and protected since we test every other week for as long as we are actively working. I don't complain about this industry much, so the only thing I really notice that I don't like is the fact that it opens so many woman up to escorting. This can expose performers to diseases and unnecessary risks. I don't do "privates" nor do I approve of them, but I can't stop other performers from doing what they want to do.

Do you watch your own scenes after you do them?

I get really excited when my stuff comes out but I mainly only watch my big scenes. I don't typically spend the extra money for my movies unless I buy them in bulk to sell to my fans!

What do you think of all the talk of "the death of porn?" I've been hearing that free porn is killing the industry for years yet websites and even DVD releases continue. Plus beautiful women continue to enter the industry and become stars!

I think we will find more ways to keep the industry going. I'm not worried at all. I don't feel like my career is at risk. If I want to continue my success in this industry I do what I can to keep myself relevant. If that means to start producing my own porn, you betcha!

Do you have better sex in your personal life or on the screen?

I keep my personal life pretty independent at this point since I have way too much going on with starting my own website. I consider my career my passion. I have better sex on screen since that is how I get my fix lately, but I have great sex anywhere. For me it's about how I feel not where I am.

Do your family and friends know about your work? If so, what do they think of it?

My mother knew before I even came out here. When I told her, all she said was it's my decision, my life, and whatever I do in life she would support me. Even though she didn't like my decision to drop out of high school like she did, she knew it was due to bullying and that I wasn't happy. I was always working after school anyways so I felt it was the perfect opportunity to go straight into a career. My best friend and I still talk. She stood by my side through all of the hard times I faced.

What advice would you have for someone else who wanted to get into porn?

I wouldn't tell anyone to get into this industry unless they were sexually, mentally, and physically prepared, and willing to test their boundaries. In high school I was constantly ridiculed for being sexually active so I knew this industry was right for me. It allowed me to express who I truly am.

How long do you plan to fuck on film?

I plan to start my own adult company, so I want to stay in this industry as long as possible. If I'm not going to be in front of the camera, then I'm going to be behind it!

Who are some other porn performers that you like? Are you up on any of the stars of the past like Kay Parker, Desiree Cousteau or Vanessa del Rio?

I don't really keep up with performers from the past, or even the present. The ones that I paid attention to are the girls that got into the industry around the same time as I did. However, since I plan to shoot girls for my own company I will be paying much more attention.

Do you diet and exercise? What sort of upkeep is required to keep your body looking as it does?

I've never really had to exercise to keep my body at the point that it is, but it's dieting that got me this way. When I first started the industry at 18 years old I was 145 pounds. Within the last two years I dropped to a healthy 120 all by eating healthier. In Minnesota we constantly ate pasta and potatoes. In California I stick to salads. I go on the occasional walk or run, but usually I'll stretch and do some yoga. Otherwise my exercise routine depends on whether I work that day or not.

Do you travel much? What are some of your favorite

places?

Yes I absolutely love to travel! Feature dancing has allowed me to travel anywhere I want to go. The place I was dying to go and was fortunate enough to be booked at was Sapphire in New York! I plan to travel all over the world from London to Hong Kong as soon as I get my passport.

What do you think about the drive to force porn performers to use condoms?

I understand the reason for condoms but personally I think it should be a choice on set that is left up to the performers. A lot of people complain about the latex and how it feels, including me.

Are you ever recognized in the streets?

When I am in California, I feel like I get recognized a lot because people aren't afraid to make it obvious that they're looking at you… but I can't tell if it's because they recognize me or just think I'm good looking. I've been recognized in an Uber and at the mall.

Would you date a fan?

I don't date at all, because I don't plan on having a relationship anytime soon. However, if I was to plan a contest or something for fans to win a chance to go out to dinner or something I would do it!

What do you have planned for the future?

There's so many opportunities for me out there! Since I model, act, and dance there is nothing that I can't do to create a substantial path for my career and my future family. At this time

I am focusing on creating my own website and company so I can last even longer in this industry!

What kind of panties are you wearing right now?

A black g string, which I plan to wear until I feel it's creamy enough to send off to a lucky fan!

Thank you very much for taking the time to do this interview. Where can readers find out more about you?

See me on Twitter, Instagram and Facebook.

Porn Star Derrick Pierce

If female porn stars are less common than they used to be, male porn stars are as rare as they have ever been. In decades of commercial porn production very few men have risen to be real stars. The best known guys like Johnny Holmes, Ron Jeremy, Peter North, Chocoball Mukai and Mandingo came up in the heyday of porn.

The list of more recent male stars seems to be limited to James Deen and Derrick Pierce. Here's what the latter had to say.

I always start out by asking the same question. How old are you and where are you from?

I'm currently 42 and I'm from western Massachusetts originally, but I moved to Los Scandalous when I was about five or so. So I'm basically from Cali.

What are your first sexual memories? What were your first sexual experiences?

First memories? I think it was having wet dreams. First sexual experience was with a girlfriend when I was like 13. I climbed 1/2 way into her room from an outdoor window while she went down on me and we had sex haha.

What was the first porn you saw? Do you still watch porn now?

First one was with Jeremy something or other and Amber Lynn. Yes I still watch porn now, but not with much frequency and never if I know the guy in the scene.

What are the skills or attributes a guy needs to do porn?

Confidence is probably the biggest thing. It's doesn't matter how big your dick is if you don't have the "balls" to go with it.

Are the risks very high? How real of a danger are things like STDs?

The risks might be higher for getting an STD compared to people outside the industry, but they are definitely lower than people who have multiple sexual partners in their private life and rarely get tested. We get tested every two weeks.

Many guys probably think you're living the dream. Obviously it is not perfect. Nothing is. What's the worst part of doing porn?

When it's good, it's *really good* and when it's bad, it's the worst thing in the world. The pressure to perform is huge. So much to think about.

How does porn continue to make money in the age of tube sites streaming full scenes in HD? Have you seen any changes since you started?

I honestly have no idea. The budgets continue to shrink for most companies.

Do you think there is any less stigma attached to men who do porn than women who do it?

Oh I think it's a total double standard. If a girls does it, she's a whore. If guys do it, it's kinda cool and high fives follow.

Do your friends and family know what you do?

Yep, most everyone knows. It's not much drama, unless it's a first date. Then I need to use caution and tact.

Do you find it more difficult to get into "regular relationships" now that you've done porn? Do you find it more difficult to get turned out by civilians or vanilla sex?

If I date a civilian, it's pretty black and white. Dating within the biz can be a bit more tricky.

What do you think about Japanese porn? How about things that spilled over from Japanese AV into the US like bukkake?

I don't really know much about the differences between the two.

What do you think about prostitution?

I think it should be legal. It's damn near the oldest profession in the world.

Thanks so much for doing this interview. Where can my readers find out more about you?

Derrickpierce.com Everything is on there. You're totally welcome!

Porn Star and Swinger Dee Siren

It might just be me or it could be due to the spread of the internet but it sure seems like more and more people are getting into making porn, swinging and the like.

Dee Siren is a swinger who bangs various guys while her husband films. Then she uploads it to the internet for the whole world to see. Who can be more interesting to talk to than her?

I usually start by asking the same question. So, how old are you and where are you from?

I'm 37 & I'm from Houston TX

Your breasts look pretty big. What size are they?

36DDD

Did you get into group sex before or after you started doing porn?

My hubby and I have been swingers for about 10 years and have been in plenty of group sex encounters before I was in porn.

How did you get into porn?

I started out as a cam model about seven years ago before it became so popular. I was always told I was too hardcore for cam and should be in porn. I was contacted by Naughty Alysha

Morgan and her hubby to shoot my first scene, "Huge Holes 15".

How does sex on video differ from having sex in private?

It is much more of a performance. My studio, sirenxxxstudios.com is focused on "real" sex so we shoot real situations rather than a set up scene. For me the biggest difference is not the sex but paying more attention to the camera than of course when there is not one around.

Can you make good money with porn?

As most businesses, there are those who want a job and those who want a career. A girl can make some good money shooting for other companies on a short term basis but if you want a long term career in the industry then most go into shooting for their own websites or owning their own studios. It is a very competitive business and it is harder now that the general idea is porn is "free" and tube sites have become mainstream.

Can you still get into vanilla sex with just one guy in private? Or do you need to spice things up now you've expanded your horizons so much?

I definitely enjoy more intimate sex with my husband & also with others if it is in private. It does not always have to be a porn scene.

Do you ever get recognized in public?

I do sometimes. I've had people just tap me on the shoulder and say they like my work, ask me if it's really me, or email me saying they saw me somewhere.

Do your friends and family know what you do?

Yes they know what I do.

What advice would you have for someone who wanted to try group sex or swinging?

Swinging and group sex is more discreet and it's good to look for a local club or group in your area where you can meet like minded people. Everyone is different and you really have to keep open communication with your partner for it to work.

How about people who want to do porn?

If you want to get into porn, of course the easiest way is to live where the work is. Which is either LA, Las Vegas, or parts of Florida. I was able to stay in Texas and build my own site and studio because my hubby and I do it together. He is the webmaster, photographer, & videographer. I am the talent. We both come up with ideas and build off of each other. It's definitely a team effort but unless you have someone to work with it's more difficult.

I see condoms in some of the scenes you do but not others. What's your opinion on rubbering up?

My studio is strictly condom only. We shoot with our fans & regular guys so we always require condoms in all our scenes. Any scenes where I have not shot with condoms are for other professional companies where all he talent are tested every 14 days. If I happen to shoot with professional male talent for my site then both he and I are both tested through Talent Testing.

What do you think about the recently defeated attempt to require condoms in California?

Even though I am an advocate for safe sex and prefer always using condoms, I do not feel it is the government's job to police the porn industry plus the bill proposed was a lot more than just about condoms. It was allowing private citizens the right to police others and profit off it. I was happy that the citizens realized it was a bad bill and it was defeated.

How often do you think about or have sexual activity?

Think about it yes because it is my business. I have sex almost daily unless there are physical reasons I can't.

Does it take up most of your time or can you turn it on and off?

I have a normal family life & have many responsibilities including raising my family and running a business so no it's not a constant. I have sex when my hubby when I want to and when I am shooting scenes for my website.

Do you still watch porn?

I am actually a doer not a watcher. I am not much into watching porn. Only on occasion.

Thanks so much for doing this interview. Do you have anything else to say to my readers?

I love all my fans and Strokers and hope to continue in this business for many years to come.

Thai Sideline Prostitute

In Asia the line between prostitution and dating can sometimes be blurred. Countless women are kept by moneyed up guys or otherwise receive compensation for dating or sex that they otherwise may or may not have participated in.

In Thailand some women have become "sideliners." They search out guys online who give them money to meet. It is a local-oriented market than many foreigners familiar only with the flashy go go bars aren't even aware of.

How old are you where are you from?

I am 25. I am from northern Thailand.

How did you get into this kind of work?

I guess it is a typical story. I needed money. My friend offered to help me out. She would post ads on sideline websites for me to find customers. The problem is that she charged me 500 Baht commission for every guy that I met.

So she was already doing it?

Yes. She was doing the work. I didn't know. I had some idea. She didn't have a regular job but I could see she had a phone and a motorbike and everything.

How did you feel the first time you met a customer?

I felt a little scared but I was also excited.

And how did it turn out?

It was good. I got money and it was fun.

How much do you get per session?

I charge 1500 Baht ($43 USD) per session. So my friend was getting 500 Baht. I was only left with 1000. Eventually it became a problem. We had a big fight and we don't even talk anymore. Now I post my own ads online.

I noticed you ask for the money up front. Most women in Thailand don't. Why do you do that?

Too many people refused to pay. After we did it they would just give me enough to pay for the hotel room. I couldn't do anything. I am just a small lady.

That's terrible. How often did that happen?

It happened many times. It was becoming too common. So I now ask for the money up front. The worst time was when the guy refused to pay but I still owed my friend 500 Baht commission. So it would have cost me money to do it that time. That's why we got into a fight.

How small are you?

I am just 150 cm (4' 11"). I weigh 42 kilograms (93 lbs).

Where do you meet customers?

They contact me after seeing my ads on sideline websites.

I mean where do you meet them in person?

I always go to love hotels. Some ask me to go to their homes but it isn't common. I won't do that. I feel it is not safe.

What if you knew them well?

If I knew them well I might consider it. But I usually only see the guys one time. I think guys who pay money for girls like to change girls a lot.

Why is that?

Because they can.

What kind of guys do you meet?

All kind of guys. Some guys are in their 20's. Some are much older.

What was the oldest guy you have been with?

He was 65.

Wow. How was he?

He was normal.

Do you only get Thai customers?

No. I had one *farang*. He didn't finish. But he gave me the money and sent me away.

How did he find you? Could he speak Thai?

Yes.

Why couldn't he finish?

He said he was drunk. I feel bad he didn't finish.

Do you want more *farang* **customers?**

I don't care really. Any guy is okay if they have money. They shouldn't be cruel either.

Could farang who don't speak Thai book a session with you?

Sure. But I don't know how. I cannot speak English.

What are your rules?

Everyone must pay first. They have to wear condom. They cannot cum in my mouth. I am not good at being on top. I can try. But I cannot do doggy style. It hurts.

So you do oral sex?

Yes. I can suck or get licked.

Do you use a condom for oral sex?

No.

Have you done anything crazy or kinky? What is the wildest thing you have done?

I met a couple for a threesome. I was so nervous. But I was excited. I wanted to try it. The lady had a sexy body. The guy was nice too. It was fun. I would do it again. Another couple contacted me but they never showed up. They lied to me.

How much did you charge for the threesome?

I charged 3000.

Did you play with the girl?

Yes. I was scared. At first I planned to just do it with the guy while she waited. But we all started to touch each other. She licked me. I did not lick her but I played with her tits and her pussy.

How long will you do this job?

Not long. Now I only do it when I need money and have free time.

What will you do in the future?

I will be an assistant nurse. I am studying for that now.

How long will you study?

The course is six months.

That sounds good. Best wishes for you now and in the future. Thanks for talking to me!

Yes. No problem. Thank you.

Thai Blowjob Bar Worker

In the first volume of *Sex Work*, I published a translation of a Japanese blowjob bar worker. Now I give you an interview with a blowjob bar worker from Thailand. While the bars are a little different in each country, they are still oriented around the same kind of service.

How old are you and where are you from?

I am old. Almost 35 already. I am from Isaan.

Are you married? Do you have any children?

I was married a long time ago. I have one daughter. She stays with my parents in Isaan.

How was your childhood?

Normal. I lived in the countryside. It was fun. The big problem was going to school. I had to go down a long dirt road. When my mom took me it was okay. One time I had to come home by myself. There were no cell phones then. I walked up the long road in the dark. I was so scared. When I got home my dad asked me how I did it. I told him I walked the road. He beat me so hard. After that I only went to school if I had a ride.

When did you start having sex?

Haha. I didn't start until I was married. I didn't know anything about sex. Boys used to come to me but I had no idea what they wanted. I used to be really beautiful. I had big boobs. Haha.

One boy used to always come to my house and whistle for me to come outside and see him. My dad heard him whistling one time and threw a rock at him. It hit him in the head. The boy didn't come anymore.

Your dad was so protective. What does he think about the work you do now?

He doesn't know what it is. Maybe he can guess. I send a lot of money home. My mom is always asking me for money. I think she gives a lot of it to my brother. He is no good. I left my motorbike at home. He rode it drunk and wrecked it. Then my mom called and told me "something happened to your motorbike." I found out what really happened last week. It is no good. I want to take care of my parents and my baby. My brother can work but he doesn't.

How long have you been working here?

Here? Not so long. A few months. But I worked in other places before. I worked at two other places.

How did you get into the work?

I needed money. My friend told me to come work in Bangkok. I saw that she had money. So I went. I didn't know what the work was but I could guess it had something to do with sex. When I came to Bangkok she brought me to work at a massage parlor on Soi 33. I didn't like it too much. One of the girls went to work in a bar like this. She told me about it and I went there.

Why do you prefer working here to working in a massage parlor?

This is so much better. I can get several customers per day. I can get money every day. I don't need to do too much. I can have sex with a customer if I want to. But I don't have to. I can just use my mouth or my hands and get money. It is easier work. I think it is safer too.

How about a go go bar or something like that?

Haha. I am not sexy enough to work there. Anyway I don't want to walk around with customers. And I don't want to go to their rooms. I don't know them. They could be crazy.

You said you have worked in a few blowjob bars. Why did you change?

I worked in the first one for many years. It was the only one I knew. Later I found out about others. The first one was really famous. There were so many girls. We used to have so many customers. There was a lot of competition but I always got customers so I didn't mind. I met a *farang* [Westerner] there. He wanted to marry me. I didn't want it but I agreed to live with him. We moved to Isaan and got a house.

How was that?

It was okay. But my daughter was scared of him. He was nice but she was still scared. He was a huge guy so he was scary for her. After I broke up with him.

Why?

Too tired of everything.

So then what did you do?

Then I came back to work in bar again. I tried another massage

230

shop. It was really no good for me. Now I am very good at blow jobs but still too tired to do massage or have husband. I just want to make money for my daughter and my family.

How do you know you are good at giving blow jobs?

Many men come to ask for me. I can do everything. I can do deep throat, face fucking, cum on face. I am not so beautiful anymore but I am better at my job than when I was young and pretty.

How many guys can you suck in one day?

I don't know. Maybe too many. Haha. Usually I have four or five customers. On good days I can have eight or nine. Sometimes I had ten.

Is that usual for all the ladies?

I don't know about all of them. Some only get one or two. We will help them get more customers if they don't have any but if I guy asks for me I must go with him. Unless he is a crazy guy then I won't. Some guys are too crazy.

What do you mean?

Some guys have problems with their minds. They are no good. I won't go with them.

How much money do you make?

I get about half of what the customer pays. At the first bar I worked I got half. Later they raised the price for customers but they didn't raise the price for us. It was not good.

How much can you make in a month?

I can make about 40,000 Baht in a month. Sometimes more. One time I made 75,000. I had a lot of tips.

Did you work anywhere before this? How much did you make?

I worked in a factory. I made 9,000 Baht a month. It was a long time ago.

Which job was better?

This one is better. That's why I work here.

How long will you work here?

As long as I can.

Macau Happy Ending Masseuse

While Macau has mostly been off the radar of English speaking people an increasing number seem to have taken notice of the vast entertainment scene there. The former colony is probably most well known for its large casinos. People from all over Asia but mainly the Chinese mainland head there every day to drop money on the tables or in the slots.

There are also a lot of adult entertainment venues such as the various sex saunas in Macau. Some are connected to casinos and large hotels but others operate on their own. While some have come and gone or changed their setups a bit the local industry seems to be holding its own even as it has been hit hard in the People's Republic. The following is an interview with a woman who worked at a well known sauna in Macau for years.

How old are you and where are you from?

I am 31. I am from a small town in Vietnam.

How long did you work in Macau?

I worked there for five years. I worked for four years then came back to Vietnam to build a house for my family. My boyfriend stopped sending me money so I went back to work in Macau again. I stayed one more year at a different sauna but when my contract finished I went back home.

What work do you do now?

I am not working. There is no work around here. I just take care of my home. My mom sells some drinks to people in the neighborhood but the money is small.

So where do you get money?

I have savings. My younger sister is working in Malaysia now. She sends money to my mom.

What kind of work does your sister do?

I don't know. I think the same kind of work like me. I told her not to go but she didn't listen.

Why did you tell her not to go?

She is not clever. She might have problems there and we cannot help her. And it is hard to get a husband if you do this kind of work. You can marry a foreigner maybe but they will not be good. Good guys don't go to saunas.

Both you and your sister got into the same kind of work. There is a lot of talk about human trafficking and the idea that many of the women working these kinds of jobs are forced or tricked into it. What do you think?

I don't know. I heard some girls got tricked to marry in China but not work. How could I get tricked? I just bought an airplane ticket and went to work. I knew I would work for my money. I got my money and that's it.

So you weren't forced or anything?

How could I be forced? I had to do everything myself. One lady around here helped me find the job. Then I went to work.

Did you know what kind of work it was?

I could guess. I am not stupid.

So what did you do in the saunas?

I did massage on the lower half of the body. But I didn't do foot massage. Only thighs and inner thigh.

Inner thigh is the way they describe penis massage right?

Haha. Yes. But we do massage the inner thigh and also the penis and the balls. It is not only a penis massage. They had that service in one sauna on a table. But that was not my job.

So did you do more regular massages or inner thigh massages?

I did both.

Where did you do the massages?

At the first place I worked we did them in the chair. I just put two big towels over the customer and slipped his shorts down the did the massage. At the second place I did the massage in a private room. The customer took off his shorts. I didn't like the second place.

How was the job in general?

It was okay. It was a job. I like Macau sometimes. There are many Chinese but I could go out at night with my friends. We had fun. I ate good food and went to party with them. Also I could learn other languages. I learned English, Mandarin and Cantonese from work.

Where did you stay?

I shared an apartment with some other Vietnamese girls. All the apartments are small in Macau.

How much money did you make?

A lot. I saved it and built a big house in my hometown. It is nice. My mom can live there and my brothers and sisters.

Can you tell me the exact amount?

It changes. You don't have the same customers every month. Usually I made 20,000 Hong Kong Dollars ($2578 USD) or more every month. Sometimes I made a lot. If I meet with a customer outside I could make a lot. And I had a boyfriend from USA. He gave me money every month.

Why did he do that?

Because he loved me. But his kids didn't want him to marry me. After a while they made him stop sending me money.

What did you do?

What could I do? I couldn't do anything. I didn't love him. He is old. But he loved me. I was happy he helped me and my family. I would marry him if I could.

You said you could make money by meeting customers. Tell me about that.

If I liked the customer I could meet him outside. Sometimes they just wanted to party. Sometimes they wanted to have sex. They would give me a nice tip.

Did you do that often?

Not so often. Only if I liked the guy.

So now you are finished with him and with working in Macau?

Yes.

So what will you do with your life?

I am looking for a husband. I want to have a baby. I am already old.

That's it?

I'm also taking care of my house and my family. What else should I do?

Also available from the Author:

Paying for Sex: A Global Guide to Prostitution

Happy Ending Massage: The Complete Report

Blowjob Bars: The Complete Report

Prostitution in Berlin: The Complete Report

Prostitution in Taipei: The Complete Report

Prostitution in Frankfurt: The Complete Report

Prostitution in Vienna: The Complete Report

Prostitution in Macau: The Complete Report

Prostitution in Jakarta: The Complete Report

www.RockitReports.com

www.ingramcontent.com/pod-product-compliance
Lightning Source LLC
Chambersburg PA
CBHW071033290526
45795CB00004B/1194